Write More!

An Intermediate Text for ESL Writers

Eileen Prince

NORTHEASTERN UNIVERSITY

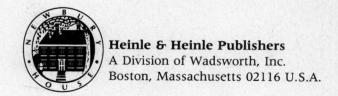

Heinle & Heinle Publishers
A Division of Wadsworth, Inc.
Boston, Massachusetts 02116 U.S.A.

To Katie, and to hope

The publication of *Write More!* was directed by the members of the Newbury House Publishing Team at Heinle & Heinle:

Erik Gundersen, **Editorial Director**
Susan Mraz, **Marketing Manager**
Kristin Thalheimer, **Production Editor**

Also participating in the publication of this program were:

Publisher: Stanley J. Galek
Editorial Production Manager: Elizabeth Holthaus
Project Manager: Rachel Youngman, Hockett Editorial Service
Associate Editor: Lynne Telson Barsky
Assistant Editor: Karen Hazar
Associate Marketing Manager: Donna Hamilton
Production Assistant: Maryellen Eschmann
Photo Coordinator: Martha Leibs-Heckly
Manufacturing Coordinator: Mary Beth Lynch
Illustrators: Taylor Oughton; Vantage Art
Cover Designer: Bortman Design Group

Photo Credits (page numbers are given in boldface): Archive Photos—**3.** UPI/Bettmann—**6.** UPI/Bettmann Newsphotos—**11.** Ron Watts—**31.** The Harwich Historical Society—**33.** Michael LaJoie—**33, 41, 42.** Dallas & John Heaton—**49.** FourByFive Inc.—**52.** RPG International—**60, 61.** Superstock—**62.** Photo Researchers/Nancy Sefton—**63.** Photo Researchers/Wayne Scherr—**65.** Popperfoto—**69.** UPI/Bettmann—**72 (top).** David King—**72 (bottom).** Irwin Blumenfeld—**78 (top).** Richard Kaplan—**78 (bottom).** Tony Stone Worldwide, Ltd./Jim Olive—**109.** Brent M. Jones—**112.** FPG International—**116 (left).** Comstock—**116 (right).** Stock, Boston/Tom Cheek—**126.** Xinhua News Agency—**158, 171 (left and right).** Culver Pictures—**212.** The Bettmann Archive—**213 (top left).** Photo Researchers—**213 (top right).** Westlight/Walter Hodges—**213 (bottom left).** Westlight/Brent Bear—**213 (bottom right).**

Heinle & Heinle Publishers is a division of Wadsworth, Inc.

Manufactured in the United States of America

Library of Congress Cataloging-in-Publication Data

Prince, Eileen.
     Write more! : an intermediate text for ESL writers / Eileen
     Prince.
          p.   cm.
     ISBN 0-8384-3405-3
     1. English language—Textbooks for foreign speakers. 2. English
     language—Rhetoric.   I. Title.
PE1128.P734   1993
428.2'4—dc20

93-27959
CIP

Contents

Acknowledgments

Great thanks for the existence of this book, and of the series of which it is a part, go to Maggie Barbieri, who suggested and encouraged both. For making certain that *Write More!* actually came into being, I thank my editor, Erik Gundersen, of Heinle & Heinle; Associate Editor Lynne Telson Barsky; and my tireless and most helpful reviewer, Peggy Armstrong, of the University of South Florida. Gratitude also goes to Rachel Youngman of Hockett Editorial Service, for shepherding the manuscript through the process of becoming a book.

I am grateful to my daughters—Deborah Nam-Krane, Suzanne, Penelope, and Katherine Nam—for their understanding, faith, and involvement. And I must finally express my gratitude to Hong, for his patience and encouragement every step of the way.

Introduction

TO THE TEACHER

Overview:

As an ESL/EFL teacher, teacher trainer, and administrator, throughout the years, I have heard a great deal of griping about writing texts for our students. I believe the reason to be that few texts actually meet the diverse needs of our students. Particularly at the intermediate and advanced levels, nonnative writers of English generally have two different types of needs: those that they share with native English writers, and those that are unique to ESL writers.

In a discussion of the writing challenges of native speakers, perhaps a need for a more academic vocabulary will be mentioned, along with such niceties of grammar as correct pronoun choice and parallel structure. Verb tense and certain types of subject-verb agreement may even be seen as specific challenges to be met and overcome. More accustomed to speaking than to writing, students may violate the rules of formal written English by slipping into the narrative present in a past context ("My friends and me are walking down the street the other day, and . . .") or by writing sentences such as, "There's these people who . . ." Many may have problems with punctuation (the comma splice and run-on sentence), and some may have difficulties with spelling. However, the main needs of most native speakers are not in the area of accuracy of form. When teachers of writing to native speakers of English talk about their students' need to write better, they are generally talking about problems with topic selection, content, sense of audience, register, organization, and so on.

ESL/EFL students, depending on their background and maturity, may share these native writer needs to a greater or lesser extent. However, what our students often require (and demand) is help in writing English correctly, particularly beyond the single sentence level. Often, when teachers of writing talk about their students' need to write better, they are talking about problems with grammar, word forms, and other formal aspects of the language in written discourse.

Write More! provides all the components necessary for an intermediate level writing course. In one book there is integrated work on content, rhetoric, and the grammar and mechanics of written English. Moreover, authentic reading passages, which can both serve as models and provide work on reading, provide springboards for writing throughout the text. These models are not just there for the students to read, although this is of course the first step in their use. Readings are accompanied by questions which encourage students to analyze the content, form, and organization of these content-rich selections.

Pedagogical Highlights

Use of pair work and small group work: Recognizing the need for audience that all real writing has, *Write More!* is organized to utilize pair work and small group work, thus freeing teachers to work on an individual basis without depriving the students of fairly immediate feedback. Moreover, editing skills are sharpened by having students gain practice in helping to edit and suggest revisions for one another's written work at various stages. Students can provide one another with ample work to revise and correct.

Ample provision for individual work: *Write More!* contains ample provision for individual work. The Portfolio of Word Forms and Exercises helps to focus on productive word-formation processes in English. The Portfolio of Grammatical Forms, Usage, and Exercises contains examples, charts, and activities to help students hone in on particular forms or usages from the different chapters. The Glossary provides definitions for some of the vocabulary in the readings. Teachers are encouraged to assign sections of the portfolios either to individual students or to the whole class, as they deem appropriate. Students who are having difficulty with particular items are encouraged to do the extra work in these sections.

Topic choice: Topic choice in *Write More!* is imposed only in a schematic way. In Chapter 3, for instance, students are asked to write about an incident that has had a great effect on their lives. Examples are given, both in the reading passages and in discussions, but the particular incident that a student selects is up to him or her. In this way, there is sufficient uniformity within the class to make it possible for the teacher to teach the group as a whole. However, topics are not so specific as to destroy a student's eagerness to write. In general, the topics offered as choices in *Write More!* and exemplified in the authentic reading passages have proven to be of high interest to students from a variety of cultural backgrounds.

Organization of the Text

Write More! contains six chapters, and is divided into two parts.

Part 1

The first part, Writing Based on Firsthand Knowledge, contains three chapters, each of which provides the material needed for a minimum of five and a maximum of ten hours of classroom instruction plus outside assignments in an intensive English program. In each chapter, students complete a short essay based on their immediate or past experience, and they are given opportunities to do more writing. Each chapter also contains other activities and exercises designed to aid students in their writing efforts.

Part 2

The second part, Writing Based on Research, contains three chapters, each providing the material needed for a minimum of ten hours of classroom instruction. Thus, each chapter in Part 2 is intended to require more time than the chapters in Part 1. The final goal of Part 2 is for the student to produce a research report or paper. The three chapters lead the student from topic selection and narrowing through various components of doing research to an actual report on a subject that he or she has selected. Writing activities leading to the final goal are provided in each of these chapters, culminating in the report or paper itself. I have been deliberately vague about the length of the project since different teachers and institutions will have different requirements. I would also suggest, where possible, allowing different students to write projects of different lengths.

The sections of chapters in Part 2 that treat research have been written to guide students through the process of doing different kinds of research, including library research. However, library research may not be practical because of a lack of facilities, or teachers may decide that library research cannot be done due to time constraints or other considerations. In this case, the text itself provides enough authentic material from original sources for students to use as the basis for their research reports. Thus, teachers will be able to make sure that students have the skills necessary to include the ideas of others in their own work, even if no actual library research is done. If desired, *Write More!* can truly stand on its own without recourse to outside sources.

ARTICULATION WITH *WRITE SOON!*

Write More! has been written as an intermediate level companion to *Write Soon!: A Beginning Text for ESL Writers. Write Soon!* leads students from paragraph writing to the simple essay, encouraging students to focus on personal experience and knowledge in their writing. Through thoughtfully interactive activities and tasks, *Write Soon!* helps students build the kind of solid foundation in writing skills that they will need to successfully master the challenges put forth in *Write More!*

TO THE STUDENT

This book will help you continue the process of becoming a more skillful writer in English. It will also provide you with information about other people and places in different parts of the world. I sincerely hope that you enjoy it.

Writing is a skill that has many uses. I invite you to write and let me know what you think of this book. Tell me what you like and what you don't like. Perhaps what you write to me will help me to make changes in future editions of this book. You can reach me in care of my publisher, Heinle & Heinle. The address is:

Eileen Prince
c/o Heinle & Heinle Publishers
20 Park Plaza
Boston, Massachusetts 02116
U.S.A.

Finally, I encourage you to follow all of your teacher's instructions in using this text. Although you will do some of your writing in the book itself, you will also need paper and something to write with. Your teacher may tell you whether you should use a pen or a pencil. You may also be told to use a typewriter or word processor to do some of your writing. Remember to follow directions, and, most of all, enjoy writing and write more!

1

Writing Based on Firsthand Knowledge

1

Childhood Memories

Prewriting focus: lists; freewriting

Rhetorical focus: past narratives

Organizational focus: pronouns; paragraph topics

Grammatical focus: *used to/would; too/enough;* spoken and
written forms

Mechanical focus: quotation marks; colons

1. THINKING ABOUT IT

Think about your childhood. Make lists of memories you have of your family, your favorite places, your personal habits, and family customs.

Focus on a particular incident or on a memory of an event that is very important to you. It may tell people about a change in your life, or it may help people to understand you better. Tell your partner about this incident, and let your partner tell you about an important childhood incident or memory. Ask each other for more details or additional information. Then, use the space below to write about it. Write for ten minutes (or however much time your teacher tells you). While you are writing, don't worry about the form or organization of what you are writing. Just continue to write without taking your pen or pencil from the paper. If you cannot think of anything to write, just write your name or another word until you can think of something.

My Memory of _____

2. READING AND REMEMBERING

About New Words: After you read this section, you can check the meanings of the difficult words in the glossary in the back of the book. You can also use the Personal Glossary at the end of this chapter to write the new words that you have learned and their definitions. There is also a Portfolio of Word Forms and Exercises, which will help you to practice using the different word forms that you may learn in this chapter. You will find sections in this Portfolio for every chapter of this book.

Dr. Richard Feynman giving a lecture

Richard Feynman was a famous physicist. He was born on May 11, 1918, and he died of cancer on February 15, 1988. In addition to being a physicist, Dr. Feynman was a talented artist and had an interest in other fields, such as history and anthropology.

In this passage, Dr. Feynman describes some of his memories of his father.

The Making of a Scientist

Before I was born, my father told my mother, "If it's a boy, he's going to be a scientist."

We had the Encyclopedia Britannica at home. When I was a small boy he* used to sit me on his lap and read to me from the Britannica. We would be
5   reading, say, about dinosaurs. It would be talking about the Tyrannosaurus rex, and it would say something like, "This dinosaur is twenty-five feet high and its head is six feet across."

What scientists think Tyrannosaurus rex looked like

*In this sentence, the pronoun *he* refers to Richard Feynman's father.

My father would stop reading and say, "Now, let's see what that means.
That would mean that if he* stood in our front yard, he would be tall enough
10 to put his head through our window up here." (We were on the second
floor.)"But his head would be too wide to fit in the window." Everything he
read to me he would translate as best he could into some reality.

Comparison of Tyrannosaurus rex and a small apartment building

It was very exciting and very, very interesting to think there were animals
of such magnitude—and that they all died out, and that nobody knew why.
15 I wasn't frightened that there would be one coming in my window as a
consequence of this. But I learned from my father to translate: everything I
read I try to figure out what it really means, what it's really saying.

*Feynman's father used the pronoun *he* to refer to a dinosaur. The encyclopedia used *it*. Why do
you think there was this difference?

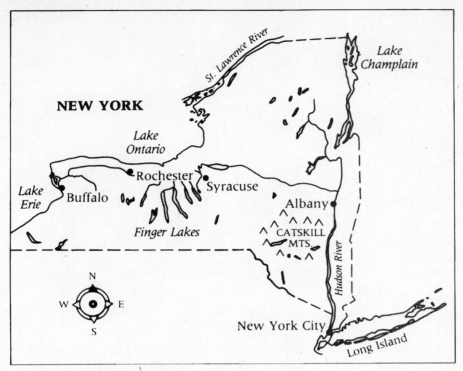

The Catskill Mountains in the State of New York

We used to go to the Catskill Mountains, a place where people from New York City would go in the summer. The fathers would all return to New York
20 to work during the week, and come back only for the weekend. On weekends, my father would take me for walks in the woods and he'd tell me about interesting things that were going on in the woods. When the other mothers saw this, they thought it was wonderful and that the other fathers should take their sons for walks. They tried to work on them but they didn't get anywhere
25 at first. They wanted my father to take all the kids, but he didn't want to because he had a special relationship with me. So it ended up that the other fathers had to take their children for walks the next weekend . . .

He was happy with me, I believe. Once, though, when I came back from MIT (I'd been there a few years), he said to me, "Now that you've become
30 educated about these things, there's one question I've always had that I've never understood very well."

I asked him what it was.

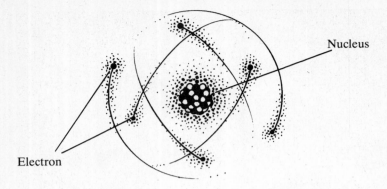

Scientists consider an atom the smallest unit of matter.

He said, "I understand that when an atom makes a transition from one state to another, it emits a particle of light called a photon."

35   "That's right," I said.

He says, "Is the photon in the atom ahead of time?"

"No, there's no photon beforehand."

"Well," he says, "where does it come from, then? How does it come out?"

I tried to explain it to him—that photon numbers aren't conserved;

40 they're just created by the motion of the electron—but I couldn't explain it very well. I said, "It's like the sound that I'm making now: it wasn't in me before." . . . .

He was not satisfied with me in that respect. I was never able to explain any of the things that he didn't understand. So he was unsuccessful: he sent

45 me to all these universities in order to find out those things, and he never did find out.

Richard Feynman with his son

A. Answer the following questions about "The Making of a Scientist" in the space provided. Do *not* look at the passage.

1. Put these sentences in order. Then look at the third paragraph of the reading to see if they are in the same order.

   a. (We were on the second floor.) _____

   b. My father would stop reading and say, "Now, let's see what that means." _____

   c. "But his head would be too wide to fit in the window." _____

d. Everything he read to me he would translate as best he could into some reality. _____

e. "That would mean that if he stood in our front yard, he would be tall enough to put his head through our window up here." _____

2. Briefly describe Dr. Feynman's relationship with his father.

_____

_____

3. What effect do you think that Dr. Feynman's father had on Feynman's becoming a physicist?

_____

_____

4. Write a brief summary of the passage. Write one paragraph which contains five sentences.

_____

_____

_____

_____

_____

_____

_____

_____

_____

5. Write one sentence which you could use to describe the most important idea of the reading passage to someone who had not read it.

_____

_____

B. Now, reread the passage on pages 7 through 10. Then, read your partner's answers to the questions in A. Complete the following checklist:

1. Are the sentences in Question 1 in the correct order? _____

2. Do you agree with your partner's answers to Questions 2 and 3? _____ If you do not agree discuss your answers and explain them to each other.

3. Compare the summaries that you each wrote for Question 4. Do they both contain the same information? If not, how are they different?

   _____

   _____

   _____

4. What about the sentences that you each wrote for Question 5? Do they contain the same information? If not, how are they different?

   _____

   _____

   _____

After you and your partner have read each other's answers and discussed them, do you want to revise any of your answers? Use a clean piece of paper to write your revised answers to the questions in A. Then, give your revised answers to your teacher.

3. LOOKING AT HOW IT'S WRITTEN

Connecting Ideas

1. Reread the second and third paragraphs of "The Making of a Scientist." Circle all the uses of *that, it, its, he,* and *his.* Then, underline the word or phrase that the pronoun refers back to (its antecedent). If there is no antecedent, write a word or phrase that you think describes what the pronoun refers to. Draw a line connecting each circled pronoun to its antecedent. Here is an example from the fifth paragraph:

   On weekends, <u>my father</u> would take me for walks in the woods and (he)'d tell me about interesting things that were going on in the woods.

2. Reread the fifth paragraph of "The Making of a Scientist." Circle all the uses of *they, them,* and *their.* Then, underline the antecedent, or, if there is none, write a word or phrase that you think describes what the pronoun refers to. Draw a line connecting each circled pronoun to its antecedent.

Understanding Grammar

◼ *Used to* and *Would*

1. Underline all examples of *used to* plus the simple form of the verb and *would* plus the simple form of the verb in the fifth paragraph. (Include '*d* in line 21.) Circle the simple past verbs in the sentences in lines 23 through 27.

2. Which forms describe past actions that occurred on a regular basis?

   the forms that contain *used to* and *would* _____

   the simple past forms _____

3. Which forms can be used to describe most past events?

   forms that contain *used to* and *would* _____

   simple past forms _____

4. Here is a rewritten version of the second paragraph of the reading. The only differences between it and the original are that the verb forms that contain *used to* and *would* have been changed to simple past or past progressive forms. Reread the original paragraph and the one below. Is there a difference in their meaning? Which version could refer to something that happened only once?

   > We had the Encyclopedia Britannica at home. When I was a small boy he sat me on his lap and read to me from the Britannica. We were reading, say, about dinosaurs. It was talking about the Tyrannosaurus rex, and it said something like, "This dinosaur is twenty-five feet high and its head is six feet across."

5. Write a description of how past forms that contain *used to* and *would* are used.

   _____

   _____

   _____

■ *Too* and *Enough*

1. Circle the word *enough* in line 9. What kind of word occurs before it?

   noun _____   adjective _____

   verb _____   adverb _____

   The chart below shows three basic forms of English verbs.

Gerund	Infinitive	Past participle
being	to be	been
going	to go	gone
having	to have	had
listening	to listen	listened
speaking	to speak	spoken

   Which form of the verb occurs after *enough* in line 10?

   gerund _____   infinitive _____   past participle _____

   If a verb comes after *enough*, is the action possible? _____

2. Circle the word *too* in line 11. What kind of word occurs after it?

   noun _____   adjective _____

   verb _____   adverb _____

   Which form of the verb occurs after the adjective?

   gerund _____   infinitive _____   past participle _____

   If a verb comes after *too*, is the action possible? _____

3. Describe how *enough* and *too* are used. In your description, say something about their meaning, and tell what kinds of words occur before and after them.

   _____

   _____

   _____

   _____

■ Punctuation

Here are six basic punctuation marks that are used in English writing, along with examples of their uses:

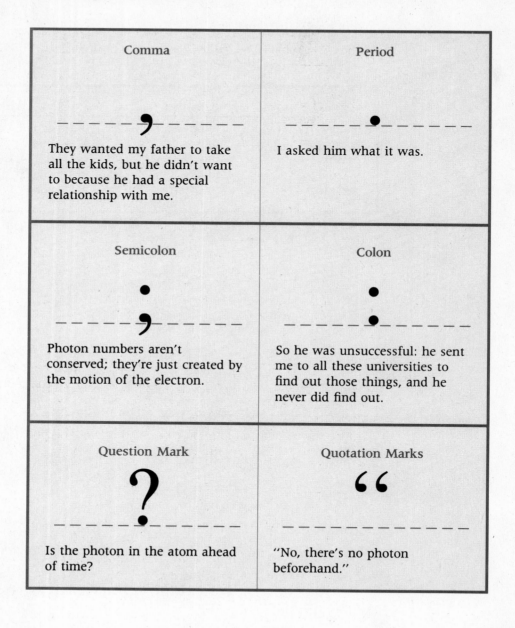

Comma	Period
They wanted my father to take all the kids, but he didn't want to because he had a special relationship with me.	I asked him what it was.
Semicolon	**Colon**
Photon numbers aren't conserved; they're just created by the motion of the electron.	So he was unsuccessful: he sent me to all these universities to find out those things, and he never did find out.
Question Mark	**Quotation Marks**
Is the photon in the atom ahead of time?	"No, there's no photon beforehand."

Now, answer these questions about some of the punctuation used in "The Making of a Scientist."

1. How many sentences are there in lines 33 through 38? _____

   What punctuation is used to show Feynman's father's exact words?

   _____

   Does a period come before or after the quotation marks? _____

2. In lines 41–42, does the quotation begin or end the sentence?

   _____

   What punctuation comes before the second set of quotation marks?

   _____

   Where does the period come? _____

3. Reread the sentences on the following lines: 16–17; 41–42; 44–46. Each of them contains a colon (:). Which of the following sentences *best* describes the function of the colon?

   It shows that what comes after it is not important. _____

   It adds an explanation to an idea. _____

   It helps to show the difference between two ideas. _____

■ Spoken and Written Forms

"The Making of a Scientist" contains examples of spoken forms that are not used in formal written English. One important difference between spoken and formal written English is in the use of tenses. In speaking, sometimes people use the present tense to describe something that happened in the past.

Find a sentence in line 36 that contains a present tense form used to describe something that happened in the past. Write the sentence in the space provided.

_____

_____

_____

_____

Now, write the sentence in correct formal written English, using a past tense verb.

_____

_____

Can you find a similar sentence in line 38? Write it in the space provided.

_____

_____

Now, write the correct formal written English equivalent.

_____

_____

Word order is also sometimes different in spoken and formal written English. Sometimes, speakers begin a sentence with an object rather than the subject of a sentence.

Underline the main verb in the following sentence from the reading:

> Everything he read to me he would translate as best he could into some reality.

Draw a circle around the phrase that is the direct object of the main verb.

Now, write the correct formal written English equivalent, beginning with the subject of the sentence.

_____

_____

4. PREPARING TO WRITE

Understanding Why

◼ Looking at the Author's Intention

1. In the reading, is there any indication about what Dr. Feynman's father did for a living? Do you think that he was a scientist? Why (not)?

_____

_____

_____

2. Why is this passage called "The Making of a Scientist"?

_____

_____

_____

3. Can you think of another possible title for the passage? Write it in the space provided.

_____

_____

Looking at Organization

■ Overall Organization: Different Kinds of Paragraphs

The first paragraph of a short essay is usually the **introduction**. It introduces the overall topic of the essay and gives the reader an idea of what to expect.

The last paragraph of a short essay is usually the **conclusion**. It lets the reader know that the essay is finished. Sometimes it repeats important ideas and events from the writing, often in different words. This kind of conclusion is a summary. Sometimes the conclusion adds a new idea to the ideas that come before it.

With your partner, study the overall organization of "The Making of a Scientist." Then answer these questions.

1. Which paragraph introduces the overall topic? _____

What is this topic? _____

2. Which paragraph contains the conclusion? _____

Is the conclusion a summary, or is there new information? _____

3. What is the purpose of most of the paragraphs?

to tell stories (narrative) _____

to compare and contrast Feynman and his father (comparison and contrast) _____

to describe where Feynman lived when he was a child (descriptive) _____

■ Narratives

The second through fifth paragraphs of the passage constitute a narrative. Each of them tells a story, or part of a story. Write one sentence that summarizes, or gives the main idea of, the paragraph.

Paragraph	Summary Sentence
2	_____ _____
3	Summary sentence: _____ _____
4	Summary sentence: _____ _____
5	Summary sentence: _____ _____

The fifth paragraph provides some details about what happened one summer when Feynman's family went to the Catskills. With your partner, complete the following chart, showing the function of each sentence in this narrative.

The Function of the Sentences in the Fifth Paragraph

Sentence	Function
1	tells the location
2	_____
3	tells what Feynman's father would do with him
4	_____
5	_____
6	_____
7	_____

■ Organizing Conversations in Written Form

With your partner, look at the sixth through thirteenth paragraphs. How does the writer use paragraphs to show who is speaking? Discuss this, and write a description of how to use paragraphs to indicate that the speaker has changed.

_____

_____

_____

_____

_____

Applying What You Have Studied

■ Putting Ideas Together

Before doing the exercises in this section, review Connecting Ideas (pages 13–14).

EXERCISE: Fill in each blank with an appropriate pronoun that refers back to the underlined word or phrase.

1. My earliest memory of <u>my mother</u> is from when I was very small. <u>She</u> was wearing high-heeled shoes and a dress that came down to <u>her</u> ankles.

2. <u>Long dresses</u> were very fashionable in those days, and my mother had a large collection of _____.

3. <u>My mother's dress</u> was quite fashionable. _____ was a copy of a Paris design.

4. My memory is quite vivid. I even remember the color and pattern of <u>the dress</u>. _____ was red and white with a wide skirt.

5. My mother was almost always with me when I was a child. I did not see <u>my father</u> so often. _____ was often away at work, and my mother and I missed _____.

6. <u>Both my mother and my father</u> were important to my early education. _____ taught me how to read, and _____ guidance was important to me.

7. My father used to play <u>number games</u> with me. _____ were a lot of fun.

8. My mother taught me <u>the alphabet</u> long before I went to school. _____ was a good teacher, so I learned _____ very quickly.

9. My mother tried to answer <u>all of the questions</u> that I asked her. _____ were sometimes silly, but she treated _____ all seriously.

10. I was fortunate because my parents and other relatives spent <u>a lot of time</u> with me when I was small. _____ was time well spent.

EXERCISE: Use the space provided to write a paragraph in which you describe an early memory that you have of one of your parents. Try to use as many pronouns as you can in your paragraph. Then, exchange paragraphs with your partner and proofread each other's use of pronouns. Return each other's paragraphs and rewrite them on clean paper. Then, give your paragraphs to your teacher.

My Memory of _____

■ Expanding Your Ideas

Use what you wrote in the previous exercise to tell a new partner about the incident that you remember from your childhood. Listen to your new partner talk about the incident that he or she remembers. Ask each other for more information and listen to each other's answers.

Try to remember some of the things that people said during the incident. Although you should try to remember their exact words, it's all right if you just guess what they were. Also, most likely the people spoke in your native language, but you are going to imagine that they spoke in English. Use the space provided to write some sentences that tell what people said. Be sure to use quotation marks and to punctuate your sentences correctly.

What People Said When _____

_____

_____

_____

_____

_____

_____

_____

_____

_____

_____

Now, write a draft in which you describe the incident and its effect on you. Be sure to include some of the things that you have told your partners about. Also, use some of the quotations that you wrote above. Use the space provided.

_____

_____

_____

_____

_____

_____

_____

_____

_____

_____

_____

_____

_____

_____

_____

_____

_____

_____

_____

_____

_____

_____

_____

_____

_____

5. WRITING MORE

Read the draft that your partner wrote on pages 24–25, and let your partner read your draft. Complete this section about your partner's draft in your partner's book. (Put your name in the blank.)

_____'s Reactions to the First Draft

1. Your first paragraph introduces the overall topic.

   yes _____   no _____

2. The essay tells where the incident took place.

yes _____   no _____

3. There are enough details.

yes _____   no _____

4. The thing I enjoyed most about reading your first draft was _____

_____

5. Please tell me more about _____ .

6. I don't completely understand the following sentences. Please explain them to me.

_____

_____

_____

_____

_____

7. I am interested in finding out more about what happened. Please try to answer these questions for me.

_____

_____

_____

_____

_____

_____

Read your partner's reactions. Then, discuss them with your partner, and let your partner discuss your questions, comments, and suggestions with you.

Rewrite your essay on a clean piece of paper, using as many new ideas from your partner as you want to. Remember that what you have written on each other's papers are *only* ideas. You don't have to follow your partner's suggestions if you don't want to, but, if you think some of the ideas will make your essay better, use them. When you are finished with your second draft, put it away.

6. WRITING IT RIGHT

Now, you are going to help your partner by *proofreading* the draft that she or he wrote in Section 4. To proofread is to read a piece of writing in order to correct errors in grammar, spelling, and punctuation. Study the parts of Portfolio of Grammatical Forms, Usage, and Exercises on pages 268–276 that your teacher tells you to study. Then, complete this section in your partner's book.

1. Are pronouns used correctly? Use this space to write any sentences that you think need to be changed.

    _____

    _____

    _____

2. Does the essay contain examples of *used to* and *would*? Are they used correctly? Use this space to write any sentences that you think need to be changed.

    _____

    _____

    _____

3. Does the essay contain examples of *too* and *enough*? Are they used correctly? Use this space to write any sentences that you think need to be changed.

    _____

    _____

    _____

4. Are colons, semicolons, and commas used correctly? Use this space to write any sentences that you think need to be changed.

    _____

    _____

    _____

5. Are past tense forms used consistently? Use this space to write any sentences that you think need to be changed.

    _____

_____

_____

6. Is the word order correct? Use this space to write any sentences that you
   think need to be changed.

   _____

   _____

   _____

   _____

**Return your partner's second draft, and take back your second draft.
Study your partner's proofreading, and ask any questions that you
may have. Then, write another draft of your essay and give it to your
teacher.**

7. WRITING IT OVER

**Read the draft that your partner wrote in Section 5. Complete this
section of your partner's book.**

1. Your essay contains a conclusion.

   yes _____   no _____

   It is a summary. _____

   It contains new information. _____

2. I enjoyed reading your essay because _____

   _____

3. I would like more information about _____

   _____

   _____

4. I don't completely understand these parts of your essay:

   _____

   _____

Give back your partner's paper, and take back your own paper. Read your partner's suggestions and think about them. Then, write another draft of your essay. Remember, you do not have to follow any suggestions unless you want to. You may also decide that you want to add or eliminate some information. Give your new draft to your teacher.

8. MORE WRITING

Follow your teacher's instructions about using this section for more practice.

1. Write about an important letter that you have received from a friend or relative. Describe the contents and purpose of the letter. Also, tell how you felt when you read it.

2. What do you hope to do or be ten years from now? Write an essay in which you describe this goal and explain who or what has caused you to want to achieve it.

3. How much influence do parents have on their children? Do you think that what our parents do when we are small can affect what we become when we grow up? Give specific examples.

4. What kinds of animals used to live on the earth? How were they different from the animals that live here today?

5. Interview one of your parents or another older relative or friend. Find out what people used to do when that person was a child. Write an essay describing how things used to be and what people would regularly do.

9. PERSONAL GLOSSARY

Use the space provided to write any words that you have learned in this chapter. Also, write a definition for each word.

_____

_____

_____

_____

2

Here and There, Now and Then

Rhetorical focus: present and past descriptions

Prewriting focus: lists; freewriting

Organizational focus: use of first and second person pronouns; showing contrast; introductions

Grammatical focus: present perfect; present perfect progressive

Mechanical focus: commas after initial adverbials

1. THINKING ABOUT IT

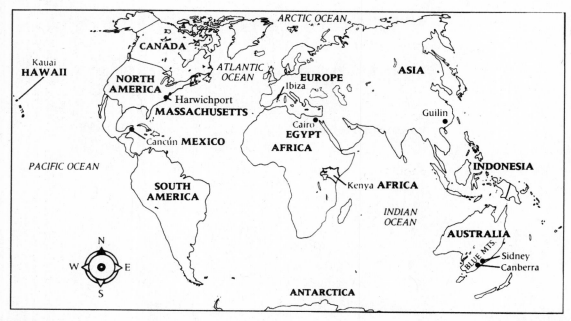

The world

Look at the photographs of the center of the town of Harwichport, Massachusetts, in the early part of this century and now. Talk with your partner about the pictures. What differences do you see?

Harwichport in the early part of this century

Harwichport, Massachusetts

Use the space provided to write about the first picture of Harwichport. Write for five minutes without stopping. Don't stop writing even if you can't think of anything to write about the picture. Just write your name or another word until you can think of something else to write about the picture.

_____

_____

_____

_____

_____

_____

_____

_____

_____

_____

_____

_____

_____

_____

_____

_____

_____

_____

_____

_____

_____

_____

_____

_____

_____

Now use the space provided to write about the second picture. Again, keep writing for five minutes.

_____

_____

_____

_____

_____

_____

_____

_____

_____

_____

_____

_____

_____

_____

Finally, write about whatever the two pictures make you think of. Use the space provided and, again, keep writing for five minutes.

_____

_____

_____

_____

_____

_____

_____

_____

_____

_____

_____

2. READING AND REMEMBERING

Cape Cod is a famous vacation area in Massachusetts. Harwichport is one of the towns on the Cape. Bonatt's Bakery and Restaurant has been located in Harwichport for more than fifty years. Read the following passage, which describes what Bonatt's was like in 1939, and what it is like today.

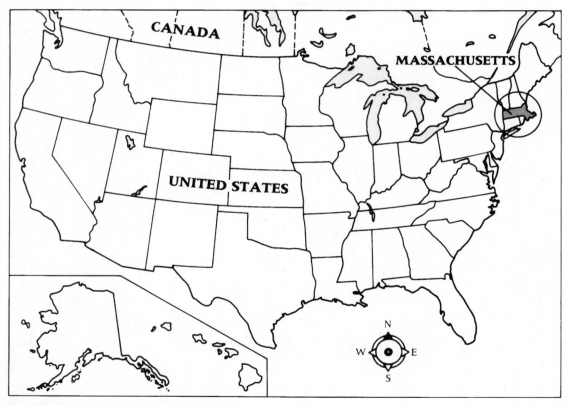

Massachusetts is one of the New England states.

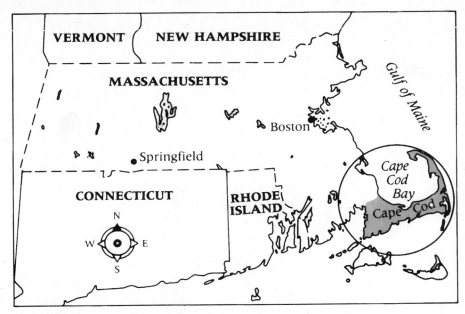

Cape Cod is a famous resort area in Massachusetts.

The Tradition Lives On

For over fifty years, Bonatt's Bakery has been serving the bakery needs of Cape Codders and summer visitors alike. Did you know that in 1939, when Bonatt's first opened its doors, it was as a restaurant, and the bakery was a very small part of the operation?

5   Bonatt's Family Restaurant took up much of the first floor of the old Bank Street location. The restaurant seated as many as fifty patrons and was run from a large kitchen area centered around a huge cast-iron stove. A.J. Bonatt and his wife, Rose, would winter at their home outside of Fall River, Massachusetts, and come to the Cape to open up the restaurant in late May, closing

10 down in mid-October. During those summer days, they would serve breakfast, lunch and dinner, six days a week.

By contrast, the bakery was a very small part of the operation. The baking was all done out of one tiny room, shared with the dishwashers on the Bank Street side of the building. Inside was a mixer, gas stove, work bench and a

15 four-pan brick oven, heated with coal (later changed over to gas). Long-time customers will remember that the front shop then consisted of two small wooden display cases and a wall case along the back; it was not enlarged until

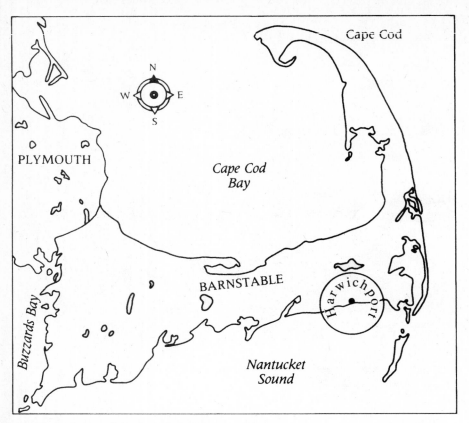

Harwichport is one of the Cape Cod towns.

the late seventies. The restaurant closed down in the early 1950's when A.J.
passed away and it became too much for Rose to run on her own. It was then that
20 Rose and her son, Jimmy, concentrated on building up the bakery business.

Now, fifty-one years later, established in our bright new home at the Port
Centre on Main Street in Harwichport, Bonatt's Bakery has grown into a
tradition in its own right and is indeed part of Cape Cod lore. Just this year,
Boston Magazine named Bonatt's as the "Best Bakery on Cape Cod."

25 What we are now most excited about is the return of the business that
began this tradition: Bonatt's Family Restaurant. We proudly continue our
pledge of excellence and the highest quality in each of our bakery products
and in every delicious restaurant menu choice as we present breakfast, lunch
and dinner for your culinary pleasure. The tradition continues, and we look
30 forward to serving you during the next fifty years!

The shore and harbors make Cape Cod an attractive place for summer visitors.

A. Answer the following questions about "The Tradition Lives On" in the space provided. Do *not* look at the passage.

1. Put these sentences in order. Then, look at the second paragraph of the passage to check your answer.

   a. During those summer days they would serve breakfast, lunch and dinner, six days a week. _____

   b. The restaurant seated as many as fifty patrons and was run from a large kitchen area centered around a huge cast-iron stove. _____

   c. Bonatt's Family Restaurant took up much of the first floor of the old Bank Street location. _____

   d. A.J. Bonatt and his wife, Rose, would winter at their home outside of Fall River, Massachusetts, and come to the Cape to open up the restaurant in late May, closing down in mid-October. _____

Bonatt's in its new location

2. Why do you think the author wrote this passage?

_____

_____

3. Whom do you think the passage was written for?

_____

_____

4. Write a brief summary of the passage. Write one paragraph which contains five sentences.

_____

_____

_____

_____

_____

_____

_____

_____

_____

_____

5. Now, write one sentence which you could use to describe the most important idea of the reading passage to someone who had not read it.

_____

_____

B. Now, reread the passage on pages 39 through 40. Then read your partner's answers to the questions in A. Complete the following checklist.

1. Do you agree with your partner's answers to Questions 2 and 3? _____ If you do not agree, discuss your answers and explain them to each other.

2. Compare the summaries that you each wrote for Question 4. Do they both contain the same information? If not, how are they different?

_____

_____

3. Do the sentences that you each wrote for Question 5 contain the same information? If not, how are they different?

_____

_____

_____

After you and your partner have read each other's answers and discussed them, do you want to revise any of your answers? Use a clean piece of paper to write your revised answers to the questions in A. Then, give your revised answers to your teacher.

3. LOOKING AT HOW IT'S WRITTEN

Connecting Ideas

■ **Beginning Sentences with Time Adverbials**

1. Check the passage to find the answer to each question.

   (line 1) **How long** has Bonatt's Bakery been serving customers?

   _____

   (line 10) **When** would they serve three meals, six days a week?

   _____

2. These phrases are called **time adverbials** because they answer questions about time (*how long? when?*). What punctuation is used after a time adverbial that begins a sentence? _____

3. What time adverbials begin the two sentences in the fourth paragraph of the passage? Write them in the space provided. Notice the punctuation.

   _____

   _____

■ **Showing Contrast**

1. The third paragraph of the passage, which begins on line 12, starts with the words "By contrast." Do these two words indicate that the reader should expect something that is similar to or different from what has come before? _____

2. Read what you wrote in Section 1 about the different photographs of Harwichport. Use your ideas to write pairs of sentences that show differences. Write your sentences in the space provided. Begin the second sentence in each pair with *By contrast*. A sample pair of sentences has been written for you.

   Example: The old Bonatt's Bakery used to stand on a corner by itself. By contrast, the new building is located between other stores.

   _____

   _____

_____

_____

_____

_____

_____

_____

Understanding Grammar

■ The Simple Present Perfect and the Present Perfect Progressive

Your class will work on this section with your teacher.

> Verbs in English sentences can consist of one or more words:
>
>   The restaurant <u>seated</u> as many as fifty patrons.
>   A. J. Bonatt and his wife, Rose, <u>would winter</u> at their home outside of Fall River, Massachusetts.

1. What is the complete verb in the first sentence of "The Tradition Lives On"? (You will need to write three words.) _____

   _____   _____

> A **present perfect progressive** verb consists of three parts:
>
>   <u>have</u> or <u>has</u> + <u>been</u> + a present participle (verb + <u>ing</u>)

2. When did the action described by the present perfect progressive verb in the first sentence begin? _____

3. Has the action finished, or is it still going on?

   _____

4. What four words describe the length of time that the action has been going on? _____ _____

_____ _____

5. What two words make up the verb in line 22? _____

_____

A **simple present perfect** verb consists of two parts:

have or *has* + a past participle

6. Does the first sentence in the fourth paragraph say that Bonatt's Bakery is still growing into a tradition or that it is finished? Does the simple present perfect verb in line 22 focus on a process that is still going on or on a result that is finished? _____

7. How would the meaning be different if this part of the first sentence in the fourth paragraph were changed to read:

. . . Bonatt's Bakery has been growing into a tradition in its own right.

_____

_____

8. Which verb form can be used to emphasize that an action started in the past and is continuing at present?

the present perfect progressive _____

the simple present perfect _____

9. Which verb form can be used to emphasize a completed state or result rather than a process?

the present perfect progressive _____

the simple present perfect _____

10. How has Harwichport changed since the early part of this century? Reread what you wrote in Section 1 about the different photographs. Use your ideas to write sentences about changes that have taken place. Write your sentences in the space provided.

_____

_____

_____

_____

4. PREPARING TO WRITE

Understanding Why

■ Looking at the Author's Intention

1. What kind of business was Bonatt's originally? Then what did it become? Why does the author have to explain that Bonatt's is now a restaurant, too? How does this relate to the title of the reading.

_____

_____

_____

_____

_____

2. In what other ways does the author describe tradition?

_____

_____

3. Why is emphasizing tradition important to the purpose of the passage?

_____

_____

4. Circle the personal pronouns that the author uses in the last paragraph. Why do you think that the author uses them? How do they make the reader feel?_____

_____

_____

_____

Looking at Organization

■ Introductions and Other Paragraphs

1. The first paragraph of "The Tradition Lives On" is the introduction. Very often, the purpose of an introduction is to get the reader's attention. What does the writer of the passage do in the introduction to get the reader's attention?

_____

_____

   Do you think that this is effective? _____

2. What does the second paragraph describe?

_____

3. What does the third paragraph describe?

_____

4. What does the fourth paragraph describe?

_____

5. What does the fifth paragraph describe?

_____

6. Which paragraph lets the reader know the purpose of the passage?

_____

7. Copy the sentence that best describes the purpose of the passage.

_____

_____

■ Two Other Passages

The author of "The Tradition Lives On" wrote the passage to make people want to visit not only Bonatt's Bakery, but also the restaurant. Because many people are interested in traditions, the fact that the Bonatt family used to have a restaurant as well as a bakery is important in the passage. However, people are also interested in new things, so the passage talks about Bonatt's "bright new home at the Port Centre."

Tourism is an important industry in most parts of the world. Many tourists enjoy visiting places that have a rich history, but they also like modern conveniences. Therefore, if you are trying to make a place seem attractive to tourists, it may be a good idea to mention tradition as well as modern conveniences. Here are two more passages that appeal to tradition and current circumstances to attract people. Read each passage, and answer the questions that follow it.

The location of Cancun, Mexico

Cancun, Mexico

Cancun, Mexico

Cancun is Mexico's paradise located along the Caribbean. Actually an island, this resort area is connected to the Yucatan Peninsula by two bridges. The waters surrounding Cancun are praised by scuba divers, and the second largest reef in the world is only a short hydroplane flight away. If you'd prefer 5 some land-based adventures, the ancient Mayan ruins of Chichen Itza, Uxmal and Tulum are a day trip away from Cancun.

You'll also enjoy the quaintness and charm of the town itself. Here you'll find excellent examples of Mexican pottery and basket weaving so you can bring a little bit of Mexico back home with you. . . . Beautiful weather and 10 luxurious resorts combine to make this vacation your best.

1. Which words in the passage show tradition?

_____

_____

2. Which words describe modern conveniences?

_____

_____

3. Which words describe natural advantages?

_____

_____

4. Would you like to go to Cancun? Why or why not?

_____

_____

Cairo: An Excerpt from an Essay by Charlie Pye-Smith

When Gustave Flaubert passed through Cairo in the 1840s, he declared: "Here the Bible is a picture of life today." In some parts of Cairo . . . this still holds true. In the narrow alleys camels and donkeys jostle with traders selling pigeons, goats, and the produce of the Nile's fertile delta.

5 However, Cairo has seen enormous changes since Flaubert's day. Certainly, much of medieval Cairo survives, but over the past 150 years the population has risen from less than half a million to over 14 million, and wave upon wave of development has transformed Cairo into a vast, pulsating metropolis.

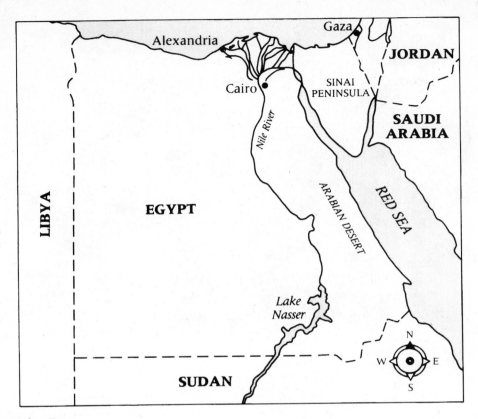

Cairo, Egypt

10   I know of no other city with such powers to thrill—and occasionally to disturb—as Cairo. Africa, Europe, and the Middle East have all brought their influence to bear on its crowded streets, and indeed it is the discordant mix of ideas and cultures that gives the city its astonishing vitality. Colorful, exuberant, and infernally noisy, Cairo provides an unforgettable introduction to the Nile and the rest of Egypt.

A busy street in Cairo

1. Which paragraph describes traditional Cairo? _____

2. Which paragraph describes modern Cairo? _____

3. Is the third paragraph a summary or does it add new ideas or information? How can you tell?

   _____

   _____

4. What pronoun begins the third paragraph? _____
   Does its use show an objective or personal point of view?

   _____

Applying What You Have Studied

■ Putting Ideas Together

Choose a city or other place that you are familiar with. Use the space provided to make a list of as many historical or traditional aspects of this place as you can. Write words, phrases, or sentences. Spend five minutes writing your list.

Historical or Traditional Aspects of _____

Now, use the space provided to make a list of as many modern aspects of the place as you can. Again, write words, phrases, or sentences, and spend five minutes writing your list.

Modern Aspects of _____

_____

_____

_____

_____

_____

_____

_____

_____

■ Expanding Your Ideas

Now, talk to your partner about the place you have written about. Answer any questions that your partner asks you. Then, listen to your partner tell you about the place that he or she has made lists about. Ask your partner questions and listen to the answers.

Use your lists and your discussion with your partner as a basis for writing the first draft of an essay about the place you have chosen. Write your draft on a clean piece of paper. Begin with an attention-getting introductory paragraph. Then, write from two to four more paragraphs. Remember that the purpose of the essay is to make other people want to visit the place. Use time or contrast adverbials to help you explain your ideas better.

5. WRITING MORE

Read the first draft of an essay that your partner wrote in the previous section, and let your partner read your first draft. Complete this section in each other's textbooks. (Put your name in the blank in your partner's book.)

_____'s *Reactions to the First Draft*

1. Your essay contains an attention-getting introduction.

   yes _____   no _____

   It makes me want to read more of the essay.

   yes _____   no _____

2. Your essay makes me want to visit the place that you have written about.

   yes _____   no _____

3. I think that it will make other people want to visit the place.

   yes _____   no _____

4. I enjoyed reading your essay because _____

   _____

5. The most interesting part of your essay is _____

   _____

   _____

6. I don't completely understand the following sentences:

   _____

   _____

   _____

   _____

7. Are you sure you need to say that _____

   _____

   _____?

8. Please write more about _____.

9. Please try to answer these questions for me:

_____

_____

_____

_____

Read your partner's questions, comments, and suggestions. Then, discuss them with your partner, and let your partner discuss your questions, comments, and suggestions with you.

   Rewrite your essay on a clean piece of paper, using as many new ideas from your partner as you want to. Remember that what you have written on each other's papers are *only* ideas. You don't have to follow your partner's suggestions if you don't want to, but, if you think some of the ideas will make your essay better, use them. When you are finished with your second draft, put it away.

6. WRITING IT RIGHT

Study the parts of the Portfolio of Grammatical Forms, Usage, and Exercises on pages 277–284 that your teacher tells you to study. Then, proofread the draft that your partner wrote in Section 5. Then, complete this section in your partner's book.

1. Do the subjects and verbs agree with each other? Use this space to write any sentences that you think need to be changed.

_____

_____

_____

2. Is the present perfect progressive used correctly? Use this space to write any sentences that you think need to be changed.

_____

_____

_____

3. Is the simple present perfect used correctly? Use this space to write any sentences that you think need to be changed.

_____

_____

_____

4. Are _since_ and _for_ used correctly? Use this space to write any sentences that you think need to be changed.

_____

_____

_____

5. Are commas used correctly in sentences that contain adverbials? Use this space to write any sentences that you think need to be changed.

_____

_____

_____

7. WRITING IT OVER

Reread your partner's latest draft. Complete this section of your partner's book.

1. I enjoyed reading your essay because _____

_____

_____

2. I would like to know more about _____

_____

_____

_____

3. Please try to answer these questions:

_____

_____

_____

_____

_____

Give back your partner's paper and take back your own paper. Read your partner's suggestions and think about them. Then, write another draft of your essay. Remember, you do not have to follow any suggestions unless you want to. You may also decide that you want to add or eliminate some information.

8. MORE WRITING

Follow your teacher's instructions about using this section for more practice.

1. Use the sentences you wrote in Section 1 to write a short essay about how Harwichport has changed.

2. Describe a store or restaurant that you enjoy shopping or eating in. Tell why you enjoy it so much.

3. Write about what you did last summer or on your last vacation.

4. Write about a place in your home town or city. Tell what it was like when you were younger and how it has changed.

5. Write a short essay for tourists who are considering visiting your home town or city or another place with which you are familiar. The purpose of your essay is to persuade them to visit this place, so try to make it sound as attractive as possible.

6. The passages that follow were written to attract tourists to visit the places they describe. Read each description. Use your dictionary to look up unfamiliar words. If you still cannot understand their meaning, ask your teacher. After you have finished reading the passages, decide which description is the most attractive to you. Which of the places that are described would you most like to visit? Finally, write a short essay in which you explain why the description made you want to visit the place.

Kenya Safari

This is the last word in exotic holiday experiences: Safari! On this journey, you'll leave civilization behind and step into the Africa of your imagination, a world where man is merely a guest in the wild kingdom of the animals. This is the Africa where "elephants pace along as if they had an appointment at the
5   end of the world" (a description from Isak Dinesen's "Out of Africa"). You'll arrive in the Kenyan capital of Nairobi, the city known to the legendary Masai tribesmen as "the beginning of all beauty." From here, you'll go off on safari—a Swahili word meaning "great expedition"—to four of Kenya's

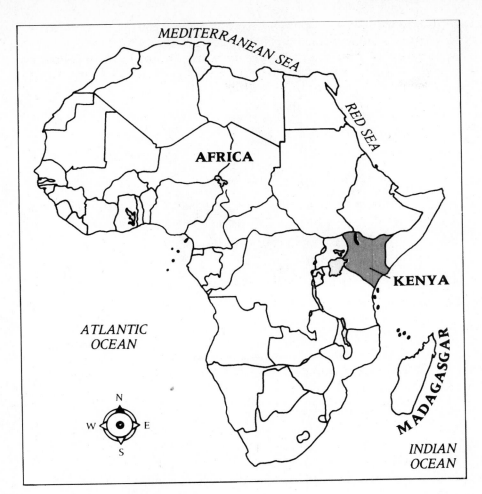

Kenya, Africa

celebrated national parks. You'll have the chance to see lions chase kudu and
impala across the acacia-dotted savanna . . . hippos frolic in the mud . . . herds
of zebra flow in waves of black-and-white . . . and leopards leap from rocky
outcrops. This is the Africa of myth and legend, where the stately giraffe
stretches as high as the sky and the lion rules as king of the beasts.

10

Animals grazing in the wild, Kenya

Sydney, Australia

Sydney, Australia's oldest and most dynamic city, offers a wide range of activities. Visitors can cruise the spectacular harbor, marvel at the beautiful scenery that winds along the coast, sample the pristine air high in the mountains or bask on one of the many beaches. At night, Sydney leaps to life,
5 opening theaters of world renown, discos for dancing till the morning's first light, and soft-lit restaurants near the water's edge. A few of its well-known landmarks are the famous Sydney Harbor Bridge, the Sydney Opera House, the Darling Harbor Complex and Centerpoint Tower.

Suggested Sights to Visit: . . .

10 **Sydney Opera House:** This prominent Sydney landmark was designed by Danish architect Jorn Utzon. Although named the Opera House, it is really a performing arts center with a concert hall, theaters for opera and drama, a cinema and recording hall. Guided tours which include dinner in the Bennelong Restaurant are available. Performance tickets are optional. . . .
15 **Blue Mountains:** Take a day tour from Sydney to see some of the most magnificent scenery in the eastern half of Australia—dramatic cliffs, deep, fern filled gorges and wide-sunken ravines. On the way there, visit Featherdale

The famous Opera House in Sydney, Australia

Animal Park. Stroll around the park and see a variety of Australian fauna—
wombats, dingos, emus, wallabies, kangaroos—and even cuddle a koala. . . .

20 **Canberra:** Canberra is Australia's capital city located approximately halfway
between Sydney and Melbourne. An international competition to design the
capital was won by the American architect, Walter Burley Griffin, in 1912. A
full-day excursion can be made from Sydney to visit this city, which is the seat
of the Australian Federal Government.

Guilin, China is a scene of natural beauty.

Guilin

Imagine a Chinese watercolor. In the foreground a lazy river rolls by. A water buffalo slowly plows a nearby rice paddy, while people crouch down, planting rice as they have for centuries. The surreal landscape is shrouded in a pastel mist. Mysterious tree-covered limestone peaks jut toward the heavens, and
5 become darker and clearer as the mist disappears in the morning sun. Meanwhile the city awakens as trishaws are peddled to market, their baskets filled with vegetables. This is Guilin.

A traditional house in the Cayman Islands

The Cayman Islands

The Cayman Islands are a peaceful place, a place reminiscent of times gone by. Most buildings are no higher than the tallest tree. The people are friendly and beaches stretch for miles. Days are filled with a host of varied activities— snorkeling offshore, sunbathing on the beach, shopping for duty-free bargains

5 or reading in a hammock hung between two palm trees. Nights are filled with calypso music playing in the background and romantic dinners overlooking a picture-perfect sunset comprised of mauve, tangerine and gold.

If you're a diving enthusiast, the Cayman Islands offer unparalleled opportunities for adventure. Miles of virgin reefs, spectacular coral canyons,

10 abundant marine life, and rarest of all, sheer coral walls that descend thousands of feet are within several hundred yards offshore. Or, if you'd prefer not to get wet, but still enjoy thrilling views of majestic marine life, take the 28-passenger Atlantis submarine ride to depths of 90 to 150 feet.

Ibiza

Sheer getaway is spelled I-B-I-Z-A. This small island of sand, sea, sun and complete casualness has some 71,000 year-round inhabitants. It looks like a cross between a Greek island and North Africa. Its name comes from Ibisos, Greek for isle of pines, but it's better known today as *la isla blanca*—the white
5 island—because all the buildings are whitewashed.

Don't look for mountains on Ibiza—look for sun-drenched beaches fringed by scarcely clad sun- and sea-worshipers who try a different beach every day, an easy task via one of the cheap local buses that run hourly. The landscape is hilly, with pine, fig, almond, olive, carob and palm trees, plus
10 vineyards and fields of vegetables and flowers sprouting from red earth.

Ibiza City was established by Carthaginians in 654 B.C. and resembles a series of white sugar cubes swarming up a hillside to the fortress and cathedral. At night Ibiza City and San Antonio Abad radiate music and exuberant fun from their many discos and cafes. More sedate is the artists'
15 colony at Santa Eulalia, whose residents include British actor Denholm Elliott and sometime author Clifford Irving.

The island's current free-spirited character stems from its raffish past. It was a hangout for artists and writers of the '20s, who brought their Bohemian lifestyle from Paris. Their spirit was renewed by another generation in the '60s.
20 Today you're apt to run into Joan Baez, Julio Iglesias, Frank Zappa, Diana Rigg, Kim Basinger or Ursula Andress.

Ibiza in the '90s is easy-going, with a daily schedule of sorts that begins with breakfast at noon, preferably at a pool or beach or on deck (either land or boat).

25 For sightseers in Ibiza City, there's the ancient Dalt Vila section, enclosed by a 16th-century wall of buff-colored stone. If you follow its narrow, cobbled streets to the old cathedral, you'll have clear views of the busy port, harbor and sea beyond. Don't miss the handsome archeological museum next door, with its displays of Phoenician and Carthaginian statues, jewelry and objets d'art
30 from the necropolis on Windmill Mound. Visit the Museum of Contemporary Art if you're interested in what local artists are doing currently.

Poipu Beach on the Kauai coast

Kauai: The Garden Island

Kauai is an unspoiled paradise of tropical wonders. Listen to the thunder of 800-foot waterfalls in Waimea Canyon. Smell the varieties of lush tropical flora in the Hanalei and Hanapepe Valleys. And feel the mist that shrouds Kauai's mountain peaks. Come play in the beautiful garden that is the oldest
5   and most majestic Hawaiian Island. A place where peace, privacy and relaxation are always in abundant supply.

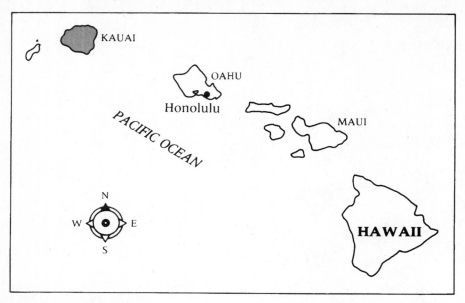

The island of Kauai, Hawaii

Experience sunny Poipu on the southern coast for exceptional beaches, snorkeling, challenging golf courses and deluxe resorts. To the east, Wailua offers 19th-century architecture and the Coconut Plantation for shopping and dining.

10 To the north, Princeville offers lush vegetation, secluded beaches and uncrowded golf courses, all overlooking the beautiful blue of Hanalei Bay.

Take to the air for the best way to enjoy the gorgeous Na Pali Coast, where cliffs plunge 4000 feet to the crashing surf below. Then take in the awesome size of Waimea Canyon, the "Grand Canyon of the Pacific," alive with the

15 jewel hues of exotic tropicals. Or cruise down the Wailua River to the famous Fern Grotto, a hauntingly beautiful cave, covered with growing ferns.

Kauai is a land of legend, of incredible beauty and of old Hawaiian ways. Escape to this enchanted land and be richly rewarded.

Indonesia

Indonesia

Indonesia, the largest archipelagic country on earth and the fifth most populous in the world, sits astride the equator across a distance equal to that from San Francisco to New York.

It is a land of stupendous variety and contrast. Tropical rainforests filled
5 with giant trees, birds of paradise and unusual orchids flourish in the shadow of towering peaks capped with eternal snow. Coral gardens the likes of which are found in only a few other places in the world lie close at the foot of the fertility of this country's volcanic soil.

This land is home to some 170 million people—a nation composed of a
10 multitude of ethnic groups yet one in outlook and in purpose, forged together by a shared historical bond that reaches back into the last millenia before the Christian Era, when the first waves of migrants crossed the waters that separate the Southeast Asian mainland from these 13,667 islands which now make up the Republic of Indonesia.

15 This was the land which merchants from Arabia and India found in the early centuries of the Christian Era in their search for spices and fragrant woods. Then the Europeans came and established their influence over these islands.

Out of that intercourse the present Indonesian nation was born. This
20 composite tapestry of people, cultures, faiths and traditions is Indonesia.

9. PERSONAL GLOSSARY

Use the space provided to write any words that you have learned in this chapter. Also, write a definition for each word.

3

Telling Stories That Make a Point

Rhetorical focus: past narratives; focusing on what is important to you

Prewriting focus: freewriting; lists

Organizational focus: chronological order

Grammatical focus: past perfect and simple past; past perfect progressive; modal perfects; result clauses with *so . . . that*

Mechanical focus: using . . . to show that words have been omitted

1. THINKING ABOUT IT

Have you ever decided ahead of time that you wouldn't like something? For example, have you ever known that you would not like a particular food even though you had not actually tasted it? What about a book or a movie? Have your tastes changed? Do you now enjoy things that you used to dislike? Choose some examples to tell your partner about.

What is prejudice? Discuss it with your partner, your other classmates, and your teacher. Give examples that you know about. Have you ever had any prejudices? Have you gotten over them? How?

Now, use the space provided to write about prejudice. Write for five minutes without stopping. Don't lift your pen or pencil from the paper. If you can't think of anything to write, just write your name or some other word until you think of something.

Prejudice

_____

_____

_____

_____

_____

_____

_____

_____

_____

_____

_____

_____

_____

_____

_____

_____

_____

_____

_____

_____

_____

_____

_____

_____

_____

_____

_____

_____

_____

_____

_____

Look at the two photographs on page 72. Do you think that some people might have been prejudiced against these people? Why (not)? Talk with your partner about one or both of the photographs. Then, use the space provided to write for ten minutes about one of them.

_____

_____

_____

_____

_____

*The great athlete
Jesse Owens with
Lutz Long*

The model Carmen

_____

_____

_____

_____

_____

_____

_____

_____

_____

_____

_____

_____

_____

2. READING AND REMEMBERING

This section contains two readings. The first, taken from "The Greater Part of Glory" by Bud Greenspan, describes what happened between African-American Olympic champion Jesse Owens and German champion Lutz Long at the Berlin Olympics in 1936. The second, "The Incident of the Hair," was written by Carmen, the model who appears in the photograph on page 72. It describes an important incident during her marriage to her husband Richard.

Read one or both of the passages in this section according to your teacher's instructions. Then, answer the questions that follow. Your teacher will tell you whether to report your answers to your partner, your group, or the whole class.

Before you read the first passage, work with your partner, classmates, and teacher to answer the following questions.

1. What are the Olympics? How often are they held?

_____

_____

2. What ideas about world fellowship do the Olympics try to encourage?

_____

_____

3. Who was Adolf Hitler? What were his ideas about non-Germans and non-whites?

_____

_____

_____

_____

4. How do you think Hitler reacted to the idea of a non-German, indeed a non-white, beating a German athlete?

_____

_____

5. Contrast Hitler's ideas with those that are encouraged by the Olympics. Which do you agree with? Why?

_____

_____

_____

_____

The German Who Helped Jesse Owens

The great Jesse Owens was frightened and confused. He stood alone at the long jump pit at the Berlin Olympic stadium on Aug. 4, 1936, trying to calm himself as Chancellor Adolf Hitler and thousands of others looked on. A day earlier, Owens had won the 100-meter final, for his first gold medal of an
5 expected four. He had won his two preliminary races in the 200 meters, and his victory in that event was a foregone conclusion. But now, in the qualifying round of the long jump, which was being contested almost simultaneously with the 200 meters, he was in trouble.

The qualifying distance to make it to the finals was only 23 feet 5½ inches.
10 Owens' world record was more than 3 feet farther than that. Earlier, wearing sweat clothes, he had tested the runway and halfheartedly leaped into the pit. Thinking it a practice run, he was amazed to learn that the judges had counted

it as his first qualifying attempt. Still upset, he overcompensated on his second attempt and fouled.

15   Now, with just one attempt left to qualify, Owens stood alone contemplating his fate. As he looked at the runway, the German champion Lutz Long—the only other entrant who'd been considered a challenge to Owens—came over and introduced himself. "Jesse," he said, "I have a suggestion: Let me put my towel a foot in front of the foul line, and use my towel as your
20 jump-off point. Then you will not have to worry about fouling." Owens agreed.

A little later, Owens came roaring down the runway and leaped magnificently, using Long's towel as his foul marker. He qualified by 2 feet.

The finals took place that afternoon. At one point, Owens and Long were tied for the lead with the exact same distance. On his fifth attempt, Owens set
25 an Olympic record. Long's last attempt failed, and Jesse had his gold medal.

As soon as Long knew he had to settle for the silver, he rushed over to the American, and they walked off the field arm-in-arm as Hitler grimly watched from his box. Long died in World War II, in 1943 in Italy; Owens died in 1980. Till the end, Jesse Owens would extol the sportsmanship of Lutz Long, saying
30 he could not have won had the German champion not come to his aid.

A. Answer the following questions in the space provided. Do *not* look at the passage.

1. Put these events in the same order that they are in in "The German Who Helped Jesse Owens."

    a. Jesse Owens set a world record for the long jump. _____

    b. Lutz Long congratulated Jesse Owens. _____

    c. Jesse Owens fouled in trying the long jump. _____

    d. Jesse Owens set a new Olympic record for the long jump. _____

    e. Jesse Owens won the 100-meter final. _____

    f. Jesse Owens died. _____

    g. Jesse Owens leaped into the pit. _____

    h. Lutz Long helped Jesse Owens. _____

    i. Lutz Long died. _____

2. Write a brief summary of what you have learned about Jesse Owens and Lutz Long. Write one paragraph which contains five sentences.

    _____

    _____

_____

_____

_____

_____

_____

_____

_____

_____

3. Now, write one sentence which you could use to describe what happened at the 1936 Berlin Olympics to someone who had not heard about it before.

_____

_____

B. Reread the passage on pages 75 through 76. Then, read your partner's answers to the questions in A. Complete the following checklist.

1. Are the events in Question 1 in the correct order? _____

2. Compare the summaries that you each wrote for Question 2. Do they both contain the same information? If not, how are they different?

_____

_____

_____

3. Do the sentences that you each wrote for Question 3 contain the same information? If not, how are they different?

_____

_____

_____

Do you want to revise any of your answers? Use a clean piece of paper to write your revised answers to the questions in A. Then, give your revised answers to your teacher.

Carmen as a young model

The photograph that Richard took of Carmen

Before you read this passage, compare the photograph of Carmen on page 72 with the two on the previous page. In which photograph do you think that Carmen is the most beautiful? Why? In which do you think she looks like a good wife? Why?

The Incident of the Hair

The world began to seep in so imperceptibly that at first I did not notice it. There was a small contretemps over the miniskirt, which was then all the rage. It was wrong for me . . . but Richard loved the new fashions and wanted to see me in them. It was too small an issue to fight over, and so I complied
5   without ever feeling comfortable or liking the way I looked. It was so insignificant, it never occurred to me that it was symptomatic of worse to come.

Our friends seemed to be racing backward in age while at the same time shouting how modern and progressive they were. . . . It seemed ridiculous. I had not wanted to be as young as they longed to be even when I was that
10   young. I thought Richard shared my opinion, but I was wrong. Youth had seduced him, and when he looked at me, he saw an older woman. He was not a deliberately cruel man, and nothing changed overnight. But change was coming.

I still have a photograph he took at about that time. In it, I'm not wearing
15   a drop of makeup. I'm still bewildered when I look at it today. How could he have thought that face was too old for him? Yet he did. There were constant remarks on the natural changes that were taking place in my body. . . . I wondered if I was being hypersensitive, if I had been a "famous beauty" for so long that I couldn't take a little kidding about being somewhat less than
20   I once was.

Then there was the incident of the hair. One morning . . . Richard reached toward me. I thought he was going to embrace me, but instead his hand moved up to my head, and he plucked out a gray hair. He studied it with an expression of horror on his face. I had been getting gray since my early
25   twenties and had lately been thinking the dyed dark hair was beginning to look hard on me. Gray is nature's way of softening at a time in a woman's life when her looks are enhanced by a softness around the face. I explained to

Richard that I wanted to see how the natural gray would look. He replied that
it would look old and awful. . . .

30   . . . I was maturing in both face and figure. It was a natural change. The
saddest part was that Richard could not recognize the compensating natural
maturing that was taking place in my heart and mind. The marriage lingered
on. I fought for it as hard as I knew how to fight, for, despite everything, I still
loved him. It was a losing battle. What was happening in the streets had
35 invaded our home, touching everything I held dear and turning it to ash.
Richard had become much too young for me. There was nothing left, and we
parted.

A. Answer the following questions in the space provided. Do *not* look at
the passage.

1. Put these events in the same order that they are in in "The Incident of the
   Hair."

   a. Carmen told Richard that she wanted to see how her hair would look if
      it were its natural color. _____

   b. Carmen and Richard got a divorce. _____

   c. Richard told Carmen that gray hair would make her look old. _____

   d. Carmen started dyeing her hair dark. _____

   e. Carmen first started getting gray hair. _____

   f. Richard plucked out a gray hair from Carmen's head. _____

   g. Carmen tried to save her marriage. _____

2. Write a brief summary of what you have learned about Carmen. Write one
   paragraph which contains five sentences.

   _____

   _____

   _____

   _____

   _____

   _____

   _____

   _____

_____

_____

3. Now, write one sentence which you could use to describe Carmen and what happened to someone who had not heard of her before.

_____

_____

B. Reread the passage on pages 79 through 80. Then read your partner's answers to the questions in A. Complete the following checklist.

1. Are the events in Question 1 in the correct order? _____

2. Compare the summaries that you each wrote for Question 2. Do they both contain the same information? If not, how are they different?

_____

_____

_____

3. Do the sentences that you each wrote for Question 3 contain the same information?

_____

_____

_____

Do you want to revise any of your answers? Use a clean piece of paper to write your revised answers to the questions in A. Then, give your revised answers to your teacher.

3. LOOKING AT HOW IT'S WRITTEN

Connecting Ideas

■ Chronological Markers

> When a piece of writing follows **chronological order,** the events are presented in the order in which they have occurred or are going to occur.

Both of the passages in Section 2 of this chapter follow a basically chronological organization. Often, when chronological organization is used, there is no need to provide connectors to mark the organization because the flow of events serves to do this.

However, when a chronological piece of writing sometimes violates that basic organization, the writer may use chronological markers to bring the reader back to the order in which the events occurred. The following are some of these chronological markers: *earlier, now, later, as soon as.*

Answer Questions 1 and 2 below by choosing either (A) or (B).

    A. "The Incident of the Hair"
    B. "The German Who Helped Jesse Owens"

1. Look at the readings in the previous section. Which one follows a more straightforward chronological organization than the other? _____

2. Which one contains chronological markers to emphasize the order in which the events occurred? _____

3. With your partner, underline the chronological connectors in "The German Who Helped Jesse Owens." Discuss why they are used.

Understanding Grammar

■ The Past Perfect and the Simple Past

> The **past perfect** consists of:
>
> *had* + a past participle

1. Which tense is used for the main verbs in the first two sentences of "The German Who Helped Jesse Owens"? _____

   Which tense is used in the third and fourth sentences?

   _____

   What about the last sentence in the first paragraph?

   _____

2. What is the time relationship between the events described with the past tense and those described in the same paragraph with the past perfect?

   Which events are earlier? _____

3. Reread the first and second paragraphs of "The German Who Helped Jesse Owens." Use the information provided by the use of the past tense and the past perfect—and any other information that you think is relevant—to put the following events in correct chronological order.

   a. Jesse Owens stood alone at the long jump pit. _____

   b. Jesse Owens won the 100-meter final. _____

   c. Jesse Owens tested the runway. _____

   d. Jesse Owens leaped into the pit. _____

   e. The judges counted Jesse Owens' jump as his first qualifying attempt.

   _____

   f. Jesse Owens was amazed to learn about the judges' decision. _____

   g. Jesse Owens overcompensated on his second attempt. _____

   h. Jesse Owens fouled. _____

4. Reread the sentences from "The Incident of the Hair" on lines 9–10, lines 10–11, and lines 17–20. Underline the past perfect verb forms in each of these three sentences. With your partner, talk about how the actions or states described by these verbs are related to actions or states described in other sentences. Why are these past perfect verb forms used?

_____

_____

_____

■ The Past Perfect Progressive

Reread the sentence that occurs on lines 24–26 of "The Incident of the Hair." The verb forms *had been getting* **and** *had been thinking* **are examples of the past perfect progressive. Why do you think that this tense is called the "past perfect progressive"?**

1. Use the space provided to write the three parts of a past perfect progressive verb. _____ + _____ + _____

2. Did the action described by these verbs begin before or after the incident that Carmen describes in the fourth paragraph? _____

   Was the action continuing at the time of the incident? _____

3. Work with your partner. Use the space provided to write a description of when to use the past perfect progressive.

_____

_____

_____

■ Modal Perfects

> A modal perfect consists of the following parts:
>
> modal + *have* + past participle

1. Underline the negative modal perfect in the following phrase from "The German Who Helped Jesse Owens."

   . . . he could not have won had the German champion not come to his aid.

2. Work with your partner to write a description of how negative modal perfects are formed.

   _____

   _____

   _____

3. Underline the modal perfect in the following question from "The Incident of the Hair."

   How could he have thought that face was too old for him?

4. Work with your partner to write a description of how modal perfect questions are formed.

   _____

   _____

   _____

■ Result Clauses with *so . . . that*

Reread the following sentences from "The Incident of the Hair":

A. The world began to seep in <u>so</u> imperceptibly <u>that</u> at first I did not notice it. (lines 1–2)

B. I wondered if I was being hypersensitive, if I had been a "famous beauty" for <u>so</u> long <u>that</u> I couldn't take a little kidding about being somewhat less than I once was. (lines 17–20)

1. In Sentence A, is the writer saying that the world began to seep in very imperceptibly or not very imperceptibly? _____

2. In Sentence B, is the writer saying that perhaps she had been a famous beauty for very long or for not very long? _____

3. In Sentence A, what was the result of the world's beginning to seep in imperceptibly?

   _____

   _____

4. In Sentence B, what was the possible result of Carmen's having been a "famous beauty" for a long time?

   _____

   _____

■ Punctuation

Using . . . to Show That Some Words Have Been Omitted

> Sometimes, we want to use someone else's words, but we do not want to use all of them. In these cases, we can write what the person said or wrote and omit some of the words. If we do this, we can use . . . to show where some words have been omitted.

Copy the sentences that contain . . . in the following lines of "The Incident of the Hair."

(lines 3–4) _____

_____

(lines 21–22) _____

_____

Discuss these sentences with your partner. What words do you think might have been omitted from them? Why?

4. PREPARING TO WRITE

Understanding Why

■ Looking at the Author's Intention

1. In both the first and second paragraphs on page 79, Carmen gives the reader the idea of future change in her relationship with Richard. In each of these paragraphs, in which sentence does she make statements to this effect?

the first sentence _____

a sentence in the middle of the paragraph _____

the last sentence _____

Why do you think that these sentences occur in this position?

_____

_____

_____

2. Carmen describes two incidents in the passage. The first is the "small contretemps over the miniskirt." The second is Richard's reaction to her gray hair. Which of these does she describe in detail?

_____

Which one is the focus of the passage?

_____

3. Bud Greenspan does not completely follow chronological order in "The German Who Helped Jesse Owens." He begins the narrative (on page 75) with Jesse Owens standing alone in the Berlin Olympic stadium. What do we learn about the athlete on the day that Greenspan first describes?

_____

_____

_____

_____

_____

Compare Owens's feelings this day with the day before.

_____

_____

_____

Would the passage have been more or less interesting if Greenspan had begun with Owens winning the 100-meter final the day before? Why?

_____

_____

_____

How else would the passage have been different if Greenspan had begun in this way?

_____

_____

_____

4. Greenspan describes what happened at the Berlin Olympics in 1936. Then, in the final paragraph, he jumps in time, first to Long's death in 1943, and then to Owens' death in 1980. Why do you think he makes these jumps rather than ending his story with Long and Owens walking off the field together? What is the purpose of the last paragraph?

_____

_____

_____

_____

Looking at Organization

■ Looking at Paragraph Functions

Focusing on a Particular Incident

> Generally, when we tell or write a story, we have a particular incident that we want to **focus** on, the one which is the most important incident in our story. Almost always, a speaker or writer spends more time or space describing this incident than others.

1. Which incident is the focus of the story in "The Incident of the Hair"?

   the argument about Carmen's wearing a miniskirt _____

   Richard's reaction to Carmen's gray hair _____

   Richard and Carmen's divorce _____

2. Which paragraph is this incident described in? _____
   Is this paragraph longer or shorter than the other paragraphs in the

   passage? _____

3. The fourth paragraph in "The Incident of the Hair" is reproduced below
   with the sentences numbered.

   > (1) Then there was the incident of the hair. (2) One morning . . .
   > Richard reached toward me. (3) I thought he was going to embrace
   > me, but instead his hand moved up to my head, and he plucked out a
   > gray hair. (4) He studied it with an expression of horror on his face.
   > (5) I had been getting gray since my early twenties and had lately
   > been thinking the dyed dark hair was beginning to look hard on me.
   > (6) Gray is nature's way of softening at a time in a woman's life
   > when her looks are enhanced by a softness around the face. (7) I
   > explained to Richard that I wanted to see how the natural gray would
   > look. (8) He replied that it would look old and awful.

   This paragraph describes the focused incident. Work with your partner and
   underline the sentences that describe what happened during this incident.
   Then, use the space provided to make a list, in chronological order, of the
   things that happened.

   1. _____

   2. _____

3. _____

4. _____

5. _____

4. Three of the sentences in this paragraph do not describe the focused incident.

   Which other sentence states the topic of the paragraph? _____

   Which sentence gives background information? _____

   Which sentence describes Carmen's feelings or beliefs? _____

Giving Background Information

> In addition to describing the incident that we want to focus on, we also provide our reader or listener with some **background information** that puts the incident in a proper context for the reader or listener to understand it. In a chronologically organized story, this background information is almost always presented before the incident is described.

Which paragraphs in "The Incident of the Hair" give background

information? _____, _____, and _____

Telling about the Result

> Often, after we have described an incident, we present information about what happened afterwards.

Which paragraph in "The Incident of the Hair" presents information about

what happened after Richard's reaction to Carmen's gray hair?

_____

Does it present information about what happened immediately afterwards

or quite a bit later? _____

The Parts of a Narrative Label the diagram which follows to show what each of the five paragraphs in "The Incident of the Hair" deals with. Use one of the following labels for each paragraph: BACKGROUND INFORMATION, FOCUSED INCIDENT, RESULT

Paragraph 1:

Paragraph 2:

Paragraph 3:

Paragraph 4:

Paragraph 5:

Analyzing "The German Who Helped Jesse Owens"

1. Which paragraphs in "The German Who Helped Jesse Owens" present mostly background information? _____ and _____

2. Which paragraphs give most of the description of the focused incident? _____ and _____

3. Which paragraphs present the results of the focused incident? _____ and _____

4. What are the first two sentences of the passage about?

   the focused incident _____

   background information _____

   What about the last sentence of the first paragraph?

   _____

   What is the effect of the author's presenting this information at the beginning, out of chronological order?

   _____

5. In the first paragraph, what tense does the author use in describing the focused information?

   the present _____   the present perfect _____
   the past _____   the past perfect _____

   What tense does he use in describing the background information?

   the present _____   the present perfect _____
   the past _____   the past perfect _____

   Why does he use these two tenses for different functions?

   _____

   _____

   _____

   _____

6. The first paragraph is the longest. It describes both background information and the focused incident.

   Which paragraph is the second longest? _____

   What does it describe? _____

■ Chronological Order

Changing Chronological Order   "The Incident of the Hair" follows chronological order for the most part, except for the third paragraph, in which Carmen talks about the present (the time when she was writing) and the past.

1. What is the topic of this paragraph?

   Carmen's hair _____

   Richard's emotions _____

   Carmen's thoughts and feelings _____

2. Why do you think that she interrupts her chronologically organized story with this paragraph?

   _____

   _____

   _____

3. Do you think that this paragraph makes her story easier or harder to understand? Why?

   _____

   _____

   _____

Using Chronological Connectors to Make the Order of Events Clear
When events are reported in the order in which they have occurred or are going to occur, there is no real need for chronological connectors, except for emphasis. For example, the following simple paragraph, adapted from the fourth paragraph of "The Incident of the Hair," does not require any chronological connectors.

> One morning Richard reached toward me. I thought he was going to embrace me, but instead his hand moved up to my head, and he plucked out a gray hair. He studied it with an expression of horror on his face. I explained to him that I wanted to see how my hair would look naturally gray. He replied that it would look old and awful.

In this paragraph, the events are presented in the order in which they occurred, so there is no need to make their order clear by using chronological connectors.

EXERCISE: The following paragraph is also based on the fourth paragraph of "The Incident of the Hair." However, the events are not presented in the order in which they occurred. Therefore, chronological connectors can serve to make their order clear. When used for this purpose, chronological connectors generally occur at the beginning of a sentence and are sometimes followed by a comma. (Why do you think that they normally occur at the beginning of a sentence and not at the end?)

For each blank in the paragraph, choose the chronological connector in parentheses that clarifies the order of events. Write the connector that you have chosen in the blank. Then, copy the paragraph in the space provided.

Richard studied the gray hair between his fingers with an expression of horror. (Earlier/Later/Two weeks ago) _____ he had reached toward me. I had thought he was going to embrace me, but instead his hand had moved up to my head. (Now/Then/Before) _____ he had plucked out a gray hair. (Earlier/ Later/Last year) _____, when I explained to him that I wanted to see how my hair would look naturally gray, he would reply that it would look old and awful.

_____

_____

_____

_____

_____

_____

_____

_____

_____

_____

_____

EXERCISE: The following paragraph is adapted from "The German Who Helped Jesse Owens." For each blank, choose the chronological connector in parentheses that clarifies the order of events. Write the connector that you have chosen in the blank. Then, copy the paragraph in the space provided.

At the Berlin Olympic stadium on August 4, 1936, Jesse Owens qualified for the long jump by 2 feet. However, it had not been easy. (Earlier in the day/Later that day/As soon as) , it had looked as if Owens was going to lose when he fouled on what the judges counted as his second attempt. When the German champion Lutz Long, who was competing against Owens, had realized that Owens was in trouble, he had put his towel in front of the foul so that Owens could use it as a jump-off point. (At one point/Shortly after that/Now)

_____, Owens had come down the runway, leaped magnificently, and qualified. (A day earlier/Till the end/Later that day) _____, Owens was going to set an Olympic record and beat Long in the finals. (Now/Then/At one point)

_____ the German champion was going to rush over to Owens and leave the field arm-in-arm with him.

_____

_____

_____

_____

_____

_____

_____

_____

_____

_____

_____

_____

_____

_____

Applying What You Have Studied

■ Putting Ideas Together

Choose an important incident in your life. Try to choose an incident that will let people know more about what you think has been important in your life. You may choose one of the following, or some other incident that was important to you:

something that happened around the
time that your life changed in some way;
a time when someone helped you when
you did not expect help;
an important sports event or other
contest that you participated in.

Tell your partner about the incident you have chosen, and let your partner ask you questions about it. Answer your partner's questions. Listen to your partner talk about an important incident. Then ask your partner questions and listen to the answers.

After your discussion, use the space provided to write a chronological list of the things that happened in the incident that you have told your partner about.

An Important Incident

_____

_____

_____

_____

_____

_____

_____

_____

_____

Use your list as an aid to writing the first draft of an essay describing the incident. Write your draft on a clean piece of paper.

■ Focusing on What Is Important to You

Giving Background Information   There is a story which goes something like this:

> A weak, thin, very old woman was walking along. All of a sudden, a strong, tall, young man ran towards her and pushed her so hard that she almost fell down.

When most people hear this story, they are horrified, particularly when the person telling it continues:

> Everyone who was watching said that the young man was a wonderful person.

What horrible people! Did this incident perhaps take place in a culture where there is complete disrespect for older people? Even in such a society (if there is one), why would a strong young person have pushed a weaker old person? You can probably come up with some other questions of your own to show your horror at this story.

Now, however, the person telling the story gives you some more information:

> The old woman was getting ready to cross a street. Although the light was with her, the young man saw a car that was going so fast that it was not going to be able to stop at the light. It probably would have killed the woman, and the way she was walking indicated that she did not see it. Therefore, he acted as quickly as he could and pushed her out of its path.

With your partner, answer these questions:

1. How do you feel about the young man now?

2. Has the *background information* that you just read changed your interpretation of what happened?

3. Has it changed your opinion of the young man?

4. Do you now understand why everyone thought he was a wonderful person?

5. Has this story helped to show the importance of background information?

Expressing Feelings or Beliefs   Bud Greenspan, the writer of "German Who Helped Jesse Owens," begins by describing how Jesse Owens felt on August 4, 1936, at the Berlin Olympic stadium. Discuss this opening with your partner. How does it affect the way you read and interpret the passage?

Now, reread the fourth paragraph in "The Incident of the Hair." Then, answer these questions with your partner:

1. How does the author's inclusion of her beliefs and feelings affect the way you feel about the incident?

2. Without the expression of feelings or beliefs, would these stories be as interesting?

3. Would you understand their importance in the life of the person they happened to?

Using Your "Camera"   In giving background information, both Carmen and Bud Greenspan describe other incidents. How much space (or how many sentences) do they use to describe these other incidents? How does this compare with the space (or sentences) they use to describe the focused incident?

Look at the photograph of Jesse Owens on page 69. With your partner, answer these questions.

1. Which part of the photograph is clearer and shows more details? (This is the part that is focused on. The other parts of the photograph are the background.)

2. Why do you think that the background is not so clear as the focused part of the photograph? Why aren't there as many details?

3. How might you interpret the photograph if all parts were focused on equally? Would it be as interesting?

Expressing a Point of View   A writer can describe an incident from his or her point of view or from the point of view of another person or other people.

When writing from his or her point of view, the writer will describe incidents using **first person** pronouns (*I/we, me/us, my/our, mine/ours*)

When writing from a different point of view, the writer will describe incidents using **third person** pronouns (*he/she/they, him/her/them, his/her/their, his/hers/theirs*).

Which of the two passages that you read in Section 2 is written from the writer's point of view? Which is written from the point of view of another person?

Reread the fourth paragraph in "The Incident of the Hair." Imagine that you were Richard at the time of the incident. Use the space provided to rewrite the paragraph from his point of view, but use first person pronouns. Be sure to change the background information and description of feelings and beliefs to show what you think Richard's point of view was. When you finish, show your story to your partner, and read your partner's story. How do they differ from the original?

Richard's Story

_____

_____

_____

_____

_____

_____

_____

_____

_____

_____

_____

Now, reread "The German Who Helped Jesse Owens." Then, without looking at the passage, use the space provided to write another description of what happened. Imagine that you were either Jesse Owens or Lutz Long at the time of the incident, and write your description from that person's point of view. (You may use your imagination to add some details, but do not change the basic story.) Use first person pronouns in your writing. Again, show your story to your partner, and read your partner's story. How do they differ from the original?

_____'s *Story*

_____

_____

_____

_____

_____

_____

_____

_____

_____

_____

_____

_____

_____

_____

_____

■ Expanding Your Ideas

Read the draft that your partner wrote on page 96, and let your partner read your draft. Complete this section about your partner's draft in your partner's book. (Put your name in the blank.)

_____'s *Reactions to the First Draft*

Overall Comments

1. I enjoyed reading your essay because _____

_____

2. The thing that I found most interesting in your essay is _____

_____

3. The part that I found most confusing is _____

_____

Background Information

1. There is enough background information for me to understand the importance of the incident.

   yes _____   no _____

2. I do not completely understand the following sentences:

   _____

   _____

   _____

   _____

3. Please give more information about:

   _____

   _____

   _____

   _____

Expression of Feelings or Beliefs

1. I think that you have expressed your feelings or beliefs in the following sentence(s):

   _____

   _____

   _____

   _____

2. I would like to know more about how you you felt about _____

   _____

"Camera" Use

1. I believe that the incident you want to focus on is _____

   _____

2. You have provided more information about this incident than about any others.

   yes _____   no _____

3. I would like to know more about the following incident: _____

   Please try to expand your description of it.

4. Perhaps you have written too much about the following thing(s):

   _____

   Please consider limiting your description of it/them.

Expression of Point of View

1. Your point of view is consistent.

   yes _____   no _____

2. You have used pronouns that correctly show your point of view.

   yes _____   no _____

3. When I read the following sentences, I was confused about your point of view:

   _____

   _____

   _____

   _____

5. WRITING MORE

Read your partner's comments. Decide what you want to change in your draft. Decide what you want to add or omit. Write another draft of your essay.

6. WRITING IT RIGHT

Study the parts of the Portfolio of Grammatical Forms, Usage, and Exercises on pages 284–297 that your teacher tells you to study. Then, proofread the draft that your partner wrote in Section 5 and complete this section in your partner's book.

1. Are the chronological connectors used correctly? Use this space to write any sentences that you think need to be changed.

   _____

2. Is the past perfect used correctly? Are the past participle forms correct? Use this space to write any sentences that you think need to be changed.

3. Is the past perfect progressive used correctly? Use this space to write any sentences that you think need to be changed.

4. Are the modal perfects used correctly? Use this space to write any sentences that you think need to be changed.

5. Is the *so . . . that* construction used correctly? Use this space to write any sentences that you think need to be changed.

Return your partner's draft, and take back your draft. Study your partner's proofreading, and ask any questions that you may have. Then, write a new draft of your essay, and give it to your partner.

7. WRITING IT OVER

Reread the draft that your partner wrote in Section 5. Complete this section in your partner's book.

1. I enjoyed reading your essay because _____

   _____

   _____

2. Please try to answer these questions:

   _____

   _____

   _____

   _____

3. Please add more information about the focused incident.

   yes _____   no _____

4. Please add more background information.

   yes _____   no _____

Give back your partner's paper and take back your own paper. Read your partner's suggestions and think about them. Then, write another draft of your essay. Remember, you do not have to follow any suggestions unless you want to. You may also decide that you want to add or eliminate some other information. Give your essay to your teacher.

8. MORE WRITING

Follow your teacher's instructions about using this section for more practice.

1. Reread the freewriting that you did on prejudice in Section 1. Use it as the basis for a paragraph or short essay.

2. In Section 1, you also wrote about one of the photographs on page 72. Use what you wrote as the basis for a short descriptive essay.

3. Reread the essay that you completed in Section 7. Then, write another essay describing the incident from someone else's point of view.

4. Find a description in a newspaper. Rewrite it as a story from the point of view of one of the people who are mentioned, focusing on the most dramatic part of the story.

5. Describe a changing relationship. Focus on an incident that makes you realize that it is changing.

9. PERSONAL GLOSSARY

Use the space provided to write any words that you have learned in this chapter. Also, write a definition for each word.

_____

_____

_____

_____

_____

_____

_____

_____

_____

_____

_____

_____

_____

_____

_____

_____

_____

_____

_____

_____

_____

_____

_____

_____

_____

_____

_____

_____

_____

2 Writing Based on Research

4

Attitudes Toward Children

Prewriting focus: choosing and narrowing a topic

Rhetorical focus: topics and comments; thesis statements

Organizational focus: connecting ideas with synonyms

Grammatical focus: infinitives and gerunds; *each* and *every*; real conditionals

Mechanical focus: choosing sources; designing a questionnaire

In this chapter, you are going to begin work on a research project. You are going to choose a topic that you will work on for the next three chapters, and you are going to begin to learn how to do research. You are also going to learn how to report information that you get from other sources. Because the purpose of this chapter is to choose a topic and begin research on it, its organization is slightly different from that of the previous chapters in this book.

1. THINKING ABOUT IT

Leaders in many countries are concerned about the size or composition of their population. Some think that they have too many people, and others think that they have too few. Some are concerned because they believe that the percentage of children and young people in their country is too low, and others worry that it is too high. In addition, many people say that the population of the whole world is too great, while others do not believe that this is a real problem.

Talk with your partner about the population level in your country or in another country with which you are familiar. Be sure to let your partner ask you questions. Answer your partner's questions. Ask your partner questions and listen to the answers. Then have your partner write some questions in the spaces provided on page 111 of your book. Write some of your questions in your partner's book. Finally, write answers after your partner's questions. If you don't know the answer to a question, write: "I don't know," or "I'm not sure, but I think that . . . ."

Here are some questions to help start your discussion:

1. Is there a population problem in _____?

2. Why do/don't you think so?

If you said yes, answer these questions:

3. Is the population of _____ too great or too small?

4. What are some of the causes of the problem?

5. What can be done about it?

If you said no, answer these questions:

3. How do you know that the population is at a good level?

4. What are some advantages to the population size of _____?

Questions and Answers about the Population of _____

1. _____
   _____
   _____

2. _____
   _____
   _____

3. _____
   _____
   _____

4. _____
   _____

5. _____
   _____
   _____

2. READING AND REMEMBERING

There are three readings in this section. The first is "The Broadnaxes: A Modern American Family." It is about a young black family who lived in Chicago when they were interviewed in 1982, and is part of an article published in *Black Enterprise*.

The second reading was published in *The Christian Science Monitor*, an important newspaper. It is titled "Japanese Leaders Lament Baby Deficit," and it describes the reaction of some Japanese politicians to their country's declining birth rate. It also shows how citizens of the same country can disagree about what is best for their nation.

The third reading is taken from an article entitled "Female Employment and Family Size among Urban Nigerian Women," by Amon O. Okpala. In the article, Professor Okpala discusses research about married women in the city of Lagos, Nigeria. The purpose of the research was to see the effects of a woman's employment situation on the size of her family and her attitudes about family size.

Do the reading(s) that your teacher assigns to you. Then, answer the questions that follow each reading. Your teacher will tell you whether to present your answers to your partner, to a group, or to the whole class.

The Broadnaxes: A Modern American Family

James's six-to-three work schedule makes him the logical parent to pick up Jeannine and take care of household chores. In return, Linda gladly does the cooking. She feels fine, though, about the heavy load of housework James carries. Since he's home before she is, she feels it's only right that he clean up the morning's chaos. James doesn't agree completely; he thinks they should share the chores more equitably, and they argue about this often. "I don't think it's fair," he says. "I hate housework as much as she does."

Another thing they both hate is the way money seems to disappear as fast as it's earned. Their combined monthly take-home pay of $1500 doesn't stretch far. Day-care is the largest single expense for them—even more than the $200 monthly mortgage payment on their small two-bedroom townhouse; more than the cost of gas and upkeep on their second-hand Buick; more than

The Broadnax family

the heating bills that, in Chicago, can be enormous; more than the $55
monthly contributions they make to a health plan insuring that both they and
15 Jeannine can see a doctor if necessary. . . .

For right now, the Broadnaxes' dreams are "on hold" while Jeannine is
growing up. Both realize it won't be long. "We're looking forward to her
starting school in a few years," says James. "Until she's a little older, I really
can't go to school at night, five nights a week. So I guess I'll just have to wait
20 a little longer."

A. Answer the following questions. Do *not* look at the passage.

1. What are James Broadnax's household duties? What are Linda's? Do they
   agree on this division?

   _____

   _____

2. What is their largest single expense? _____

3. When will James start going to school?

   _____

4. Imagine yourself at a party, introducing James Broadnax to someone who
   does not know anything about him. Complete the following introduction
   with one or two sentences.

   I'd like you to meet James Broadnax. _____

   _____

   Now, imagine youself introducing Linda Broadnax to someone who does
   not know anything about her. Complete the following introduction with
   one or two sentences.

   I'd like you to meet Linda Broadnax. _____

   _____

5. Write a brief summary of the passage. Write one paragraph which contains
   five sentences.

   _____

   _____

   _____

   _____

_____

_____

_____

_____

_____

_____

6. Now, write one sentence which you could use to describe the most important idea of the reading passage to someone who had not read it.

_____

_____

7. This article was written in 1982. What do you think the Broadnax family is like today?

_____

_____

8. What effects do you think having one child had on the Broadnaxes' lives?

_____

_____

Do you think their lives would have been better or worse without a child? Why?

_____

_____

Would they have been better or worse off with more than one child? Why?

_____

_____

_____

B. Reread "The Broadnaxes: A Modern American family." Then, read your partner's answers to the questions in A. Complete the following checklist.

1. Do you agree with your partner's answers to Questions 1–3? If you do not agree discuss your answers and explain them to each other.

agree _____   disagree _____

2. Compare the way you and your partner would introduce James and Linda Broadnax to people who did not know them. What are the similarities in your introductions?

_____

_____

_____

What are the differences?

_____

_____

_____

3. Compare the summaries that you each wrote for Question 5. Do they both contain the same information? If not, how are they different?

_____

_____

_____

4. Compare the sentences that you each wrote for Question 6? Do they contain the same information? If not, how are they different?

_____

_____

_____

5. Compare your answers to 8. What are the similarities?

_____

_____

_____

_____

What are the differences?

_____

_____

_____

_____

After you and your partner have read each other's answers and discussed them, do you want to revise any of your answers? Use a clean piece of paper to write your revised answers to the questions. Then, give your revised answers to your teacher.

Japanese Leaders Lament Baby Deficit

Japan's largely male political leadership, often charged as being sexist, has stepped up its lament that young women are not having enough babies to ensure the survival of the Japanese race.

"There is a mood [in Japan] to enjoy life, rather than giving birth and
5 suffering," said Hideyuki Aizawa, director-general of the Economic Planning Agency, at a private meeting of politicians last week.

"Many Japanese women have entered university and taken a job and that will lead them to marry late and have a shorter time for having babies," he added.

In June, feminists both in Japan and abroad criticized a remark allegedly
10 made by Finance Minister Ryutaro Hashimoto that the nation's declining birth rate was caused in part by allowing women to go to university. He denied having made the comment.

Officials had predicted that a steady decline in the fertility rate, the average number of children that a woman bears in a lifetime, would end in

A traditional Japanese family

A young Japanese couple

15 1987. But it has continued to drop, reaching 1.57 children. That rate is below the level needed to keep the population from falling.

Earlier this year, the Health and Welfare Ministry predicted that if the present low rate persists, the number of Japanese would drop to only 45,000 by the end of the next millennium.

20 "At every wedding reception that I have attended," said Mr. Aizawa, "I speak out and say that if this excellent Japanese tribe is on its way to becoming extinct, then I cannot die easily."

The ruling Liberal Democratic Party (LDP) is considering a tax break on the costs of giving birth, but officials doubt that such incentives will be enough 25 to persuade people to start having more children.

Rather than citing women as the problem's cause, many experts have said that high housing costs and the rigors of Japan's education system have discouraged young people from having families, and that people no longer rely on children for care in their old age.

30 Government officials feel constrained from taking action because of residual memories among Japanese of a prewar propaganda campaign that almost ordered women to have children.

"The issue of a declining birthrate is up to each person's life desires, and so it is very difficult to come out with any policies," says Takeo Nishioka, 35 chairman of the LDP's general affairs council and a former education minister.

He contends that Japan would be better off if married couples had five children each, but that "may be impossible, so three may be better."

Mr. Nishioka also worries that as more and more women enter the work force, mothers are not attending enough to the home education of their 40 children. "It's time for people to think about raising children by themselves," he says.

A. Answer the following questions in the space provided. Do *not* look at the passage.

1. What does the article say that some of Japan's political leadership is afraid of?

_____

_____

2. What do some members of the leadership believe to be the cause of the problem? What different causes are cited by many experts?

_____

_____

_____

3. What did Japanese Finance Minister Ryutaro Hashimoto allegedly say? Which group has criticized him for this?

   _____

   _____

4. What does the former education minister, Takeo Nishioka, worry is happening as more and more Japanese women enter the work force?

   _____

   _____

5. This passage was written by an American writer. Do you think a Japanese writer might have said similar things? Why (not)?

   _____

   _____

6. Write a brief summary of the passage. Write one paragraph which contains five sentences.

   _____

   _____

   _____

   _____

   _____

   _____

   _____

   _____

   _____

7. Now, write one sentence which you could use to describe the most important idea of the reading passage to someone who had not read it.

   _____

   _____

8. Do you think that the fears of the Japanese political leadership are justified? Why (not)?

   _____

   _____

B. Reread "Japanese Leaders Lament Baby Deficit." Then, read your
partner's answers to the questions in A. Do you agree with your
partner's answers to Questions 1–5 and 8? If you do not agree discuss
your answers and explain them to each other. Finally, compare the
summaries that you each wrote for Question 6. Do they both contain the
same information? If not, how are they different? What about the sentences that you each wrote for 7? Do they contain the same information?

**After you and your partner have read each other's answers and
discussed them, do you want to revise any of your answers? Use a
clean piece of paper to write your revised answers to the questions.
Then, give your revised answers to your teacher.**

**The next reading is part of a report that Dr. Amon O. Okpala wrote
about a study of Nigerian women who live in cities. He wanted to see
if there is a relationship between what kind of work a woman does in
addition to caring for her family and the size of her family. In his
study, Dr. Okpala divided the women he interviewed into three
groups. Scan his description of the three categories and underline the
name of each category.**

Female Employment and Family Size among Urban Nigerian Women

The civil service category includes women working in all government
ministries and corporations, and it embraces all types of activities from clerical
and teaching jobs to managerial positions. I grouped women working in
government ministries or corporations into one category, because they are all
5   under the same work rules, that is, the same conditions of service and fringe
benefits, and are consequently under the same work regime.

The category for the self-employed includes different varieties of economic
activities performed by women. These activities may be either petty trading,
medium-scale trading, or sewing. Self-employed women are usually referred
10 to as businesswomen in Nigerian society, and the common factor among them
is the fact that they are not bound by any employer's work rules. Consequently, they can be very flexible with their work time schedule.

The third category includes women who are housewives. They are usually
not engaged in any type of formal economic activity outside the home. In
15 some instances, as I observed during the interview, some housewives are
engaged in economic activities around the house. Such activities usually range
from hairdressing to other minor petty-trading activities which are very small
in scale and are centered around the home.

Which group do you think will have life styles that make it difficult to raise children? Which two groups do you think will be more similar to each other with respect to raising children? Here is what Okpala predicts.

---

20 Of these three categories it is expected that the economic activities performed by women in the first category may tend to be incompatible with child rearing. The reason is that the work regime of civil servants is quite formal. Therefore, the fertility levels of women employed in the civil service sector will be quite low relative to the other categories. For the self-employed businesswomen, one would expect that their activities,
25 although performed away from home, might not be incompatible with child rearing. Therefore, their fertility level may not be too different from that of women who are housewives.

Did your predictions agree with what Okpala wrote?

The women who participated in Okpala's study were asked to answer questions on a questionnaire. Write your answers to these three questions that they were asked:

1. Is bearing children the most important thing a woman can do? _____

2. A husband and wife have five daughters and no sons and wonder if that is enough children. If you are in such a position, will you have more children?

   _____

3. What do you think is the best number of children to have? _____

Read your partner's answers and discuss your answers with each other. Then, complete the following table to show what you think each group of Nigerian women answered.

Answers Given by Each Group			
Question	Civil Servants	Self-employed	Housewives
(1)			
(2)			
(3)			

Do you think that a woman's age affected her answers?

The following tables show how the different categories of women answered the three questions. They also show how different age groups responded.

Table 1   Fertility Attitudes in Lagos, 1983: Selected Responses of Housewives (N = 142)

		Response by Age Group in Percentages				
Question	Response	15–21	22–28	29–35	36–42	43–49
Is bearing children the most important thing a woman can do?	Agree	76	78	79	74	81
	Disagree	24	22	21	26	19
A husband and wife have five daughters and no sons and wonder if that is enough children. If you are in such a position, will you have more children?	Yes	95	78	86	87	95
	No	5	22	14	13	5
What do you think is the best number of children to have?	1–3	5	2	0	0	5
	4	14	13	0	3	0
	5	14	23	17	0	9
	6	10	5	7	16	14
	7	7	8	10	10	5
	8+	0	0	0	3	5
	Up to God	52	50	66	68	62
Total number of respondents by age group		21	40	29	31	21

Table 2   Fertility Attitudes of Married Women in Lagos, 1983: Selected Responses of Businesswomen . . . (N = 152)

Question	Response	Response by Age Group in Percentages				
		15–21	22–28	29–35	36–42	43–49
Is bearing children the most important thing a woman can do?	Agree	78	57	74	75	82
	Disagree	22	43	26	25	18
A husband and wife have five daughters and no sons and wonder if that is enough children. If you are in such a position, will you have more children?	Yes	78	71	76	78	82
	No	22	29	24	22	18
What do you think is the best number of children to have?	1–3	22	9	4	2	0
	4	45	17	10	2	0
	5	0	6	6	2	5
	6	0	17	12	33	5
	7	0	14	6	3	22
	8+	0	3	10	6	5
	Up to God	33	34	52	32	63
Total number of respondents by age group		9	35	50	36	22

Table 3   Fertility Attitudes of Married Women in Lagos, 1983: Selected Responses of Civil Servants . . . (N = 294)

Question	Response	Response by Age Group in Percentages				
		15–21	22–28	29–35	36–42	43–49
Is bearing children the most important thing a woman can do?	Agree	64	72	53	65	52
	Disagree	36	28	47	35	48
A husband and wife have five daughters and no sons and wonder if that is enough children. If you are in such a position, will you have more children?	Yes	64	48	51	57	33
	No	32	52	49	43	66
What do you think is the best number of children to have?	1–3	4	5	10	0	7
	4	29	37	22	16	26
	5	10	21	21	25	22
	6	18	18	21	14	11
	7	4	1	2	6	7
	8+	0	0	1	4	7
	Up to God	36	19	23	35	19
Total number of respondents by age group		28	97	91	51	27

Here is Okpala's description of the results shown in the tables.

Tables 1 through 3 illustrate the findings of the fertility attitudes of Lagos married women. An examination of the three tables will show that
30   except in one instance for each age group a higher percentage of housewives than other respondents agree that childbearing is the most important thing a woman can do. For housewives, on the average about 78 percent of all respondents agree that childbearing is the most important thing a woman can do, while the average of all who agree for the
35   self-employed women is 73 percent and for civil servants 61 percent. This result is not at all surprising, because one would expect the civil servants, who are relatively more educated, to find other fulfillments in life besides childbearing.

The answers to the question concerning the family with five daughters
40   and no son (which was meant to examine the importance of a male child to the respondents) were as expected. Housewives once again consistently show a greater degree of male-child importance than the rest for each category. For the age group from 15 to 21, 95 percent of all interviewed housewives agree that they will have more children if they find themselves in the condition
45   specified in the second question on Table 1, while only 78 percent of the businesswomen and 64 percent of the civil servants who responded to the same question agree. This remarkable result is found with every age group. For the question concerning the best number of children to have, an average of over 50 percent of the housewives respond that the issue is up to God to
50   decide. A lesser percentage of the businesswomen and civil servants agree that the decision is up to God.

A. Answer the following questions. Do *not* look at the passage.

1. What three categories of married women are dealt with in the study?

   _____

   _____

   _____

2. Which group has the most time to spend with their children? Which group has the least time? Why?

   _____

   _____

   _____

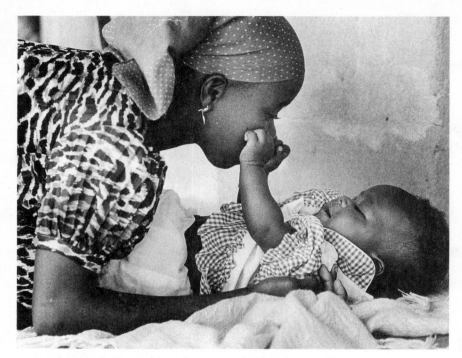

Nigerian mother and child

3. Do any of the groups think that having children is not important? Which group thinks that it is the most important?

_____

_____

_____

4. Write a brief summary of the differences in the three groups' beliefs about having children. Write one paragraph which contains five sentences.

_____

_____

_____

_____

_____

_____

_____

_____

_____

_____

_____

5. Now, write one sentence which you could use to describe the most important idea of the reading passage to someone who had not read it.

_____

_____

B.   Reread "Female Employment and Family Size." Then read your partner's answers to the questions in A. Complete the following checklist.

1. Do you agree with your partner's answers to Questions 1–3? If you do not agree discuss your answers and explain them to each other.

2. Compare the summaries that you each wrote for Question 4. Do they both contain the same information? If not, how are they different?

_____

_____

_____

3. Compare the sentences that you each wrote for Question 5. Do they contain the same information? If not, how are they different?

_____

_____

_____

After you and your partner have read each other's answers and discussed them, do you want to revise any of your answers? Use a clean piece of paper to write your revised answers to the questions. Then, give your revised answers to your teacher.

3. LOOKING AT HOW IT'S WRITTEN

Connecting Ideas

■ Using Synonyms

In the Passages:

1. What synonym for "household chores" appears in line 3 of "The Broad-naxes: A Modern American Family"? _____
Where else do the words "chores" and "housework" appear in the first paragraph of this passage? _____

2. What synonyms for *expense* can you find in the second paragraph?
_____, _____,
_____, and _____

3. In line 9 of "Japanese Leaders Lament Baby Deficit," the author talks about "a remark" that was criticized by feminists. What word in line 12 is a synonym of *remark*? _____

4. What noun phrase does the phrase "such incentives" in line 24 refer back to? _____

EXERCISE: Fill in each blank with a synonym or words with a similar meaning to the underlined word or phrase that comes in the earlier sentence. The first one is done for you.

1. I disagree with what that politician said. However, her remarks were quite interesting.

2. I think it is important to let people know what you think. That way, you can learn their opinions about your _____.

3. We should respect our mothers and fathers. After all, we owe a lot to our
_____.

4. It takes a lot of help for a child to truly become an adult. Without assistance, it is difficult to really _____.

5. In developed countries, microwave ovens and dishwashers have made housework much easier. Without these _____, it would take much longer to feed a family.

Understanding Grammar

■ Infinitives and Gerunds

1. The following clause from "Japanese Leaders Lament Baby Deficit" (line 15) is written in the present perfect:

> But it has continued to drop . . .

Compare it to the same clause rewritten in the future tense, using *will*:

> But it will continue to drop . . .

Which verb is different?

   has continued _____   to drop _____

   Which is the main verb? _____

   What are verb forms like *to drop* called?

   gerunds _____   infinitives _____

2. Rewrite this sentence from "The Broadnaxes: A Typical American Family." Use the past progressive.

> We're looking forward to her starting school in a few years.

   _____

   Which verb changes?

   are looking foward to _____   starting _____

   Which is the main verb? _____

   What are verb forms like *starting* called?

   gerunds _____   infinitives _____

3. Reread the following paragraph from "Japanese Leaders Lament Baby Deficit."

> In June, feminists both in Japan and abroad criticized a remark allegedly made by Finance Minister Ryutaro Hashimoto that the nation's declining birth rate was caused in part by allowing women to go to university. He denied having made the comment.

In the second sentence, which action came first: Finance Minister

Hashimoto's denial or his (supposedly) making the comment? _____

   _____

4. Verb forms such as *having made* are called **perfect gerunds**.

A perfect gerund consists of two parts:

Having (the gerund form of *have*) + a past participle

When can you use a **perfect gerund?**

to show that the action described by the perfect gerund took place *before*

the action described by the main verb _____

to show that the action described by the perfect gerund took place *after*

the action described by the main verb _____

5. In the sentence that occurs in lines 7–8 of "Japanese Leaders Lament Baby Deficit," what is the object of the verb *will lead?*

_____

6. Fill in each blank in these phrases from "Japanese Leaders Lament Baby Deficit."

a. (line 11) by _____ women to go to university

b. (line 16) to _____ the population from

_____

c. (lines 27–28) have discouraged young people from _____

families

d. (line 30) constrained from _____ action

e. (line 40) to _____ about

_____ children

When a verb form is the object of a preposition, it must be a

(gerund/infinitive) _____.

7. Reread this sentence from lines 8–9 of "Female Employment and Family Size." Underline the gerunds.

> These activities may be either petty trading, medium-scale trading, or sewing.

What part of speech do the gerunds in these sentences function as?

nouns _____

verbs _____

prepositions _____

■ *Each* and *Every*

Reread sentences and clauses in the following passages. Then, answer the questions that follow.

> "Japanese Leaders . . . ": 20; 33
>
> "Female Employment . . . ": 30–31; 47

1. Which word emphasizes individuality more?

each _____

every _____

2. Which word has a meaning similar to *all?*

each _____

every _____

■ Future Real Conditionals

In "Female Employment and Family Size," one of the questions that Okpala asks is:

> If you are in such a position, will you have more children?

1. What time is Okpala referring to in this question?

the present _____

the past _____

the future _____

Which verb occurs in the main clause?

are _____

will have _____

Which occurs in the subordinate (*if*) clause?

    are _____

    will have _____

2. In sentences about the future, which tense is used in the main clause?

    the present _____

    the future _____

Which tense is used in the subordinate clause?

    the present _____

    the future _____

4. PREPARING TO WRITE

Understanding Why

■ Looking at the Author's Intention

1. There are many quotations in both "Japanese Leaders Lament Baby Deficit" and "The Broadnaxes: A Typical American Family." In your opinion, why did the authors use so many quotations?

_____

_____

How would the passages be different if there were no quotations?

_____

_____

2. In the last excerpt from "Female Employment and Family Size" (lines 28–51), only some details from the three tables are discussed. What are they?

_____

_____

_____

Why do you think that Okpala chose to discuss these details and not others?

_____

_____

_____

Looking at Organization

■ Newspaper Articles

"Japanese Leaders Lament Baby Deficit" is taken from a newspaper,
The Christian Science Monitor.

1. Do newspaper readers usually have a lot of time to spend on each article or

   just a little? _____

   Where is the most important information in the article found?

   at the beginning _____

   in the middle _____

   at the end _____

2. Why do you think that newspaper articles are organized in this way?

   _____

3. Reread the summaries of this article that you and your partner wrote on
   page 118. Is their organization similar to that of the article or is it different?

   _____

   Why do you think that you wrote your summaries in this way?

   _____

   _____

   _____

■ *Another*

1. Which words in the first sentence of the second paragraph of "The Broadnaxes: A Modern American Family," connect this paragraph with the first paragraph?

   Another thing they both hate _____

   the way money seems to disappear as fast as it's earned _____

   What is the topic of the first paragraph that these words refer back to?

   _____

   Which words give the new information that is the topic of the second paragraph?

   Another thing they both hate _____

   the way money seems to disappear as fast as it's earned _____

2. When *another* is used, what is the minimum number of people or things that are being talked about? _____

■ Organizing According to Category

1. "Female Employment and Family Size" is an article from a scholarly journal. In lines 1–18 how many categories of married women does the author describe? _____

   How many paragraphs are in this section? _____

2. In which part of each paragraph is the category defined?

   the beginning _____

   the middle _____

   the end _____

3. In which part does the author explain the reason(s) for grouping married women into each category?

   the beginning _____

   the middle _____

   the end _____

4. Do the paragraphs in this section all have the same organization? _____

   Why do you think that the author organized this section in this way?

   _____

   _____

Applying What You Have Studied

■ Choosing a Topic

Choosing Something to Learn More About   In this chapter, you have discussed and read about several different topics. Among them are population size, family size, women and employment, the high cost of raising children, and government control of population. Can you think of any other topics that are related to what you have read about or discussed in this chapter? What are they?

_____

_____

_____

_____

Which topic that you have discussed, read about, or listed above interests you the most? Choose only one.

_____

_____

Why does this topic interest you the most? Use the space provided to write for five minutes about why it interests you. Don't lift your pencil from the paper, and don't stop writing. If you can't think of anything to write, just write your name or the topic over and over again until you have something to write. If you need more space, continue to write on a piece of paper.

Why I Am Interested in _____

_____

_____

_____

_____

_____

_____

_____

_____

_____

_____

_____

_____

_____

_____

_____

Narrowing a Topic   Topics can be broad (general) or narrow (specific). For example, "population" is a very broad topic. "Population size" is narrower, but it is still quite broad. "The size of the population in a specific country" is a narrower topic.

EXERCISE: **Work with your partner to rank each group of topics from the broadest to the narrowest. (If there are any words that you do not understand, ask your teacher or use your dictionary.) The first one is done for you.**

1. married women/women/married women with children

   women; married women; married women with children
   _____

2. professors/economics professors/teachers

   _____

3. science/biology/anatomy

   _____

4. prime ministers/political leaders/the Prime Minister of Japan

   _____

5. cooking/household chores/making dinner

   _____

6. mortgage payments/expenses/monthly bills

   _____

7. learning/college education/formal education

   _____

8. civil service jobs/Nigerian women's jobs/teaching

_____

9. working at home/economic activities/working

_____

10. how many children to have/decisions/choices a family must make

_____

With your partner, decide whether the topic you wrote about on pages 135–136 is narrow enough. If you decide to narrow it further, write your narrower topic in the space provided.

_____

_____

■ Commenting on a Topic

Many sentences can be divided into two parts: a topic and a comment. Here is an example:

The birth rate in Japan is declining.

Draw a circle around the topic of this sentence. Underline the comment.

1. Which part of the sentence describes what is being talked about?

   the topic _____

   the comment _____

2. Which part of the sentence adds information?

   the topic _____

   the comment _____

In many English sentences, the topic is the subject and the comment is what traditional grammarians call the predicate (the verb and all of its complements). However, particularly in sentences that contain a comment that is a point of view, **the topic is not always the subject of the sentence.** In context, **topics are usually old information, and comments are usually new information.** Another way of saying this is that **the topic is what a sentence is about, and the comment is what we say about the topic.**

Draw a circle around the topic of each sentence. Underline the comments.

My Japanese friend believes that the size of the population of Japan is not a problem.

There is a relationship between a Nigerian woman's employment situation and the size of her family.

Write a new sentence that contains a different comment about the size of the population of Japan.

_____

_____

Write another sentence that contains a different comment about the relationship between a Nigerian woman's employment situation and the size of her family.

_____

_____

EXERCISE: Draw a circle around the most likely topic in each of the following sentences. Underline the comments.

1. The birth rate in Japan is not decreasing.

2. Some Japanese political leaders think that the birth rate is much too low.

3. According to some feminists, there was a sexist remark made by one of Japan's leaders.

4. It may be housing costs and the Japanese educational system that are causing young people to have fewer children.

5. James and Linda Broadnax both work full time.

6. What James hates most is cleaning when he gets home from work.

7. Day-care is the largest monthly expense for the Broadnaxes.

8. Nigerian women who work in the civil service tend to want smaller families.

9. Nigerian housewives may engage in economic activities around the house.

10. There are three categories of women in Okpala's study.

EXERCISE: With your partner, write sentences that contain comments on each topic.

1. The cost of raising children

   _____

2. The ideal family size

   _____

3. Husbands and wives

   _____

4. Women who work

   _____

5. Education

   _____

■ Asking Questions about a Topic

When you begin to get more information on a topic, you will not know everything that you are going to learn about it. Therefore, rather than thinking of a sentence that contains a topic and a comment, you may think of a question that asks about a possible comment on a topic. For example, Question A can lead to two different sentences that contain two different comments, and Question B can lead to many different sentences containing many different comments:

Question A: Is there a relationship between men's jobs and the size of their families?

leads to:

Sentence 1: There is a relationship between men's jobs and the size of their families.

or:

Sentence 2: There is no relationship between men's jobs and the size of their families.

Question B: What is the relationship between men's jobs and the size of their families?

leads to:

Sentence 1:

or:

Sentence 2:

or

Sentence 3:

or:

.

.

.

.

EXERCISE: Use the space provided to write questions about the topic that you narrowed on page 137.

_____

_____

_____

_____

_____

_____

Read your partner's questions and let your partner read your questions. Can you add any questions about your partner's topic? Use the space provided in your partner's book to write some additional questions.

Additional Questions

_____

_____

_____

_____

■ Planning Research

Deciding Which Sources to Use   Many people are frightened by the idea of doing research. They think it is boring. They have heard that it is a difficult process that requires going to a library and reading books that no one has looked at for a long time. Actually, research can be both interesting and easy. It is interesting when its purpose is getting information or answers to questions that the researcher wants to know about. It is easy when, because of knowing what he or she is looking for, the researcher also knows what kind of research to do or where to look for the information or answers.

You will have to do some of your research by reading books and articles in books, magazines, newspapers, or scholarly journals. However, one of the most interesting types of research is finding out what people do or think about a particular situation. This type of research often involves reading newspapers or watching news programs for reports of what people (especially important political leaders) have said recently, or observing what one or more people do and asking them about it, or setting up a questionnaire to see how a group of people feels about something.

Which of the readings that you did in Section 1 of this chapter was based on each of the following sources? Write a one- or two-sentence description of how the author of each reading used the sources.

1. Speeches or statements by political leaders

    Article: _____

    How the author used the sources: _____

    _____

2. Observing what one or more people do and asking them about it

Article: _____

How the author used the sources: _____

_____

3. Setting up a questionnaire to see how a group of people feels about something

Article: _____

_____

How the author used the sources: _____

_____

Reread the work that you did on pages 135 and 137 to narrow your topic and the questions that you and your partner wrote about it on pages 140 and 141. Use the space provided to make a list of the different types of sources that you can use to try to get more information about your topic and to answer your questions.

_____

_____

_____

_____

_____

_____

Read your partner's list, and let your partner read your list. Can you help each other with any more ideas about possible sources?

Designing a Questionnaire   If you or your partner has chosen a questionnaire as one of your possible sources, work together to answer the following questions, which will help you in designing your questionnaire. If neither of you has chosen a questionnaire, work with one of your classmates who has.

Questions to Answer Before Designing a Questionnaire

1. What kinds of people do you want to ask about their opinions? (for example, what age range, what sex, what profession(s), etc.)

   _____

   _____

2. What topics do you want to ask their opinions about?

   _____

   _____

3. What are some questions that can help you to learn their opinions?

   _____

   _____

   _____

   _____

   _____

Most people do not like to answer long questions, and many people become confused if questions are not specific enough. They may also become angry if you assume they have a certain opinion and then ask about it. Therefore, when you write a questionnaire, you must make your questions as short and specific as possible. However, remember that questions that are *too* specific are also too long. (One way of making your questions specific is by giving your subjects choices.) You must also avoid presupposing any opinions for your subjects. Do not tell them what to think. It also helps if you can relate your questions to the lives or experience of your subjects.

EXERCISE: With your partner, choose the question in each pair that would be better to ask on a questionnaire and underline it. Then, give your reasons for choosing it.

1. Since children are very important in a marriage, what is the smallest number of children that you think a married couple should have?

   Which is the smallest number of children that a married couple should have?   0   1   2   3   4   5   more than 5

   _____

   _____

2. Which is more important: a woman's education or her raising children?

   Should a married woman who has a one-year old child begin to study at a university?

   _____

   _____

3. If a husband and wife both work, should they share the housework?

   If a husband and wife both work, who should do the housework? the husband   the wife   both the husband and the wife   someone else

   _____

   _____

4. What is the best age for a woman to get married? For a man?

   Since we know that it is important to limit our population, and since we know that the age at which people get married affects the size of their families, what do you think is the best age for a woman to get married? For a man?

   _____

   _____

5. How much responsibility should the schools have for educating children? How about the parents?

Who should be responsible for teaching children to read?
their parents   the schools

_____

_____

If you are going to use a questionnaire, use the space provided to write some questions that you may decide to use in it. Ask your partner and other classmates to answer them. If any of the questions are not specific enough, if they are confusing or too difficult, or if they presuppose the subject's opinion, rewrite them or substitute other questions.

Possible Questions for My Questionnaire

_____

_____

_____

_____

_____

_____

Beginning Research   The topic you have chosen in this chapter will be the topic that you research and write about in this chapter and in Chapters 6 and 7. In this chapter, your research will consist of finding out what people do or think about your topic. Look at the list of possible sources that you made on page 142. If you decided to write a questionnaire, look at the possible questions that you wrote on this page. Your teacher will tell you how much time you have. Use that time to consult the sources that you listed and to write and begin to use the questionnaire that you have designed (if you have chosen to use this source). Remember to keep careful records. If you get information from a newspaper, magazine, or radio or television show, write down all of the information listed in the following chart:

What to Write Down About Information from a Newspaper, Magazine, or Radio or Television Show

—Full name of the newspaper, magazine, or show

—Title of the article or specific segment of the show

—Date on which the article was published or the show was aired

—Volume in which the article appeared

—Place in which the newspaper or magazine is published, or place and station from which the show is aired

—Name of the author(s) or show host(s)

—Pages on which the article appeared

—Specific page(s) on which the material you are using appeared

If you administer a questionnaire to someone, you will not need the person's name. (Many people feel more comfortable if they do not have to give their names.) However, you may need the following information (and any other information that you may want to use to categorize your subjects later).

Information That May Be Needed about People Who Answer a Questionnaire

—Age

—Sex

—Profession

—Number and ages of children

—Marital status (married, single, or divorced)

—How long married or divorced

—Location of home (name of city or town)

Some people prefer to keep information about what they have read or learned from their questionnaire subjects on index cards. Others prefer to keep it in a notebook. Still others prefer to keep in in a computer file. It doesn't matter where you keep your information, as long as you keep it in a place where you can find it easily whenever you need it.

■ Thesis Statements

Paragraphs and Topic Sentences

A **topic sentence** is a sentence which tells what a paragraph is about. It usually states the writer's point of view (or comment) as well as the topic. Although many books tell beginning writers to put the topic sentence at the very beginning of a paragraph, it may occur at any place. In fact, there may not be a topic sentence. However, the reader will usually be able to create one for a particular paragraph.

EXERCISE: With your partner, read the following paragraphs, and underline the topic sentence in each one. If the paragraph does not contain a topic sentence, write one.

1. Many Japanese political leaders are concerned about the causes of the declining birth rate in their country. Hideyuki Aizawa, the director-general of the Economic Planning Agency, believes that this problem is caused by women's marrying late because of jobs and education. Others attribute the problem to the high cost of housing and the Japanese education system.

   _____

2. The second paragraph of "The Broadnaxes . . ."

   _____

3. The third paragraph of "The Broadnaxes . . ."

   _____

4. The first paragraph of "The Broadnaxes . . ."

   _____

5. Amon O. Okpala administered a questionnaire about attitudes toward family size to three groups of married Nigerian women. One of the questions was: "A husband and wife have five daughters and no sons and wonder if that is enough children. If you are in such a position, will you have more children?" Among young women, the differences in how the three groups answered this question were quite striking. For housewives from 15 to 21, ninety-five percent said that they would have more children. Seventy-eight percent of businesswomen in this age group gave the same answer. However, only sixty-four percent of civil servants in this age group replied in the affirmative.

Longer Works and Thesis Statements

Whereas a topic sentence gives the main idea of one paragraph, a thesis statement gives the main idea of a longer work. Thesis statements are helpful to writers as well as to readers. They help beginning writers to remember what the focus of their writing is. If thesis statements are chosen according to the length of a work, they also help to guarantee an appropriate amount of information.

A thesis statement indicates the amount of information that a writer will be expected to provide.

EXERCISE: With your partner, decide how much support would be needed for each of the statements below. What kind of support would be good? Then decide for which of the following the statement would be best as a thesis:

short essay (3–5 paragraphs)
longer essay (10 or more paragraphs)
research paper (10–20 double-spaced typed pages)
chapter in a book

Write your ideas and decision after each statement.

1. My brother and I have different ideas about when people should get married.

   _____

   _____

2. The number of children that the women in my country want to have is related to several different factors.

   _____

   _____

3. The reasons that many people in developed countries want to have only one child are complex.

   _____

   _____

4. Family size is influenced by different factors in developed countries and in developing countries.

   _____

   _____

5. Family income has a complex relationship with the number of children that people want to have.

   _____

   _____

6. The women's movement has caused American women's attitudes about working to change greatly since 1970.

   _____

   _____

7. Men's ideas about family size are influenced by their beliefs about the role of women.

   _____

   _____

8. Although my job takes away from the time that I have to study, it gives me a great deal of pleasure.

_____

_____

9. Women in developed countries have more opportunities than women in developing countries.

_____

_____

10. Studies have shown that children who have a great deal of contact with adult family members grow up to be more confident.

_____

_____

Do you think it is always possible for writers to choose their thesis statements before beginning their research?

yes _____

no _____

Which part of a thesis statement do you think writers are likely to decide on after they do their research?

the topic _____

the comment _____

■ Expanding Your Ideas

In Chapters 5 and 6, you are going to write a research report or paper on the topic that you chose in Section 2 (or on another topic if you wish to change). In this chapter, you are going to write a short essay that explains the importance or interest of that topic.

Since you are going to spend a great deal of time studying and writing about your topic, it is important for you to be sure that it is something you want to learn more about. Begin by reviewing what you wrote about why your topic is interesting on pages 135 and 136. Discuss it with your partner, and discuss what your partner wrote. Do you still want to work on this topic? If not, you can choose another one.

After you are sure which topic you want to write about, write another first draft of a short essay in which you explain why your topic is important or interesting. You may give some personal reasons, but be sure also to explain why the topic is generally important or interesting.

5. WRITING MORE

Read the draft that your partner wrote about why his or her topic is important or interesting, and let your partner read your draft. Complete this section about your partner's draft in your partner's book. (Put your name in the blank.)

_____'s *Reactions to the First Draft*

1. The thing that I liked the most about your essay is _____

   _____

2. Your essay has convinced me that your topic is interesting.

   yes _____   no _____

3. If you write more about _____, you may attract people's interest more.

4. I think that you may make your topic more exciting by answering the following questions:

   _____

   _____

   _____

   _____

Read your partner's questions, comments, and suggestions. Discuss them with your partner, and let your partner discuss your questions, comments, and suggestions with you.

   Rewrite your essay on a clean piece of paper, using as many new ideas from your partner as you want to. Remember that what you have written on each other's papers are *only* ideas. You don't have to follow your partner's suggestions if you don't want to, but, if you think some of the ideas will make your essay better, use them. When you are finished with your second draft, put it away.

6. WRITING IT RIGHT

Study the parts of the Portfolio of Grammatical Forms, Usage, and Exercises on pages 298–309 that your teacher tells you to study. Then proofread your partner's second draft and complete this section in your partner's book.

1. Perfect infinitives and gerunds
   Use this space to write any sentences that you think need to be changed.

   _____

   _____

   Use this space to suggest other sentences in which your partner can use perfect infinitives or gerunds.

   _____

   _____

   _____

2. Gerunds as nouns
   Use this space to write any sentences that you think need to be changed.

   _____

   _____

   _____

   Use this space to suggest other sentences in which your partner can use gerunds as nouns.

   _____

   _____

   _____

3. "Empty" *it* as the subject of sentences that contain infinitives
   Use this space to write any sentences that you think need to be changed.

   _____

   _____

   _____

Use this space to suggest other sentences in which your partner can use "empty" *it* as the subject of sentences that contain infinitives

_____

_____

_____

4. *Each* and *every* as third person singular forms
Use this space to write any sentences that you think need to be changed.

_____

_____

_____

Use this space to suggest other sentences in which your partner can use *each* and *every*.

_____

_____

_____

5. Present real conditionals
Use this space to write any sentences that you think need to be changed.

_____

_____

_____

Use this space to suggest other sentences in which your partner can use present real conditionals.

_____

_____

_____

6. Future real conditionals
Use this space to write any sentences that you think need to be changed.

_____

_____

_____

Use this space to suggest other sentences in which your partner can use future real conditions.

_____

_____

_____

7. Past real conditionals
    Use this space to write any sentences that you think need to be changed.

_____

_____

_____

Use this space to suggest other sentences in which your partner can use past real conditionals.

_____

_____

_____

8. Synonyms to connect ideas
    Use this space to write any sentences that you think need to be changed.

_____

_____

_____

Use this space to suggest other sentences in which your partner can use synonyms to connect ideas.

_____

_____

_____

Discuss your suggestions with each other. Then, return your partner's draft, and take back yours. Study your partner's proofreading, and ask any questions that you may have. Then, write another draft of your essay.

7. WRITING IT OVER

Read your partner's last draft. Complete this section in your partner's book.

1. I enjoyed reading your essay because _____

_____

_____

2. Please answer these questions for me:

_____

_____

_____

_____

3. These sentences confuse me. Can you make them clearer?

_____

_____

_____

_____

4. I think it would be a good idea for you to _____

_____

_____

_____

Give back your partner's paper and take back your own paper. Read your partner's suggestions and think about them. Then, write another draft of your essay. Remember, you do not have to follow any suggestions unless you want to. You may also decide that you want to add or eliminate some other information.

8. MORE RESEARCH

1. If you have created a questionnaire, continue to give it to subjects and begin to tabulate the results.

2. Try to spend part of every school day doing research on the topic that you chose on page 150. As you do your research, be sure to write down the following information about each source that you use: the name(s) of the author(s) or editor(s); the date of publication; the title of the book or article; the title of the magazine or journal in which an article is found; the place of publication; the name of the publisher; the pages on which an article is found; the pages on which you have found specific information or a quotation.

3. Find a journal article in your field of interest. Write about the type of research that was included in it.

9. PERSONAL GLOSSARY

Use the space provided to write any words that you learned in this chapter. Also, write a definition for each word.

5 Men and Women at Work

Rhetorical focus: different types of introductory paragraphs; different types of concluding paragraphs

Organizational focus: different relationships between ideas; thesis statements; outlining; using tables and graphs

Grammatical focus: the passive voice; reduced adjective clauses that contain present and past participle adjectives

Mechanical focus: modifying quotations; using dashes

1. THINKING ABOUT IT

With your partner or group, discuss working in your country or in another country. Do most men and women work? What about women who have children? Can both men and women hold the same jobs? Do they receive the same salaries?

Use the space provided to write for five minutes about what you have said and heard. Compare and contrast the positions of men and women in the work force of the country you have spoken about or one of the other countries that you have discussed.

The Positions of Men and Women in the Work Forces of _____

_____

_____

_____

_____

_____

_____

_____

_____

_____

_____

_____

_____

_____

_____

_____

_____

_____

Rejoin your partner or group. Tell each other about the topic that you began doing research on in Chapter 4. Explain why your topic is interesting or important. Ask each other questions. Use the space provided to write more about your topic. If the position of men and women in the work force is related to your topic, write something about the connection.

2. READING AND REMEMBERING

There are four readings in this section. The first is part of an article entitled "A Tribute to the Household: Domestic Economy and the Encomienda in Colonial Peru," by Enrique Mayer. *Encomienda* is a colonial term from Latin America. It means a group of Indians *given* to a Spaniard by the king or queen. The Spaniard to whom this group belonged was entitled to take labor and goods from it. He was called the *encomendero*. Dr. Mayer's essay contains an imaginary interview with some of the Peruvian Indians who were part of the *encomienda* of a Spaniard named Juan Sanchez Falcon. The passage that is used here is called "Paying Tribute to the Encomendero: An Indian's Point of View."

The second reading—Female Employment in Western Europe—comes from an article entitled "Workforce Europe: Are Women Coming in from the Cold?," by Rebecca Rolfes. In it, the author describes the kinds of jobs that women tend to hold in western Europe.

The third reading is taken from an article in *The China Business Review* called "Holding up the Sky." It talks about how recent changes in the Chinese economy have affected the position of women in the work force. The title of the article comes from a saying by Mao Tse-Tung: "Women hold up half the sky."

The fourth reading is the longest. It is entitled "Women and the Labor Market: The Link Grows Stronger." It describes the changing participation of women in the American work force and makes predictions about what will happen in the future.

Your teacher may assign you to read one or more of the passages. Before you do any reading, discuss these questions with your partner:

Which of these four readings do you think will interest you the most?

Why?

Which if any do you think may contain information related to the topic that you chose in Chapter 4?

What makes you think so?

Use the space provided to compare and contrast your answers to these questions with your partner's.

_____

_____

_____

_____

_____

_____

_____

_____

After you finish the reading(s) that your teacher has assigned to you, complete the questions that follow. Your teacher will tell you whether to report your answers to your partner, a group, or the whole class.

Paying Tribute to the Encomendero: An Indian's Point of View

Sure! I spend almost half a year working for the encomendero, although it seems to me that it is all the time. Take spinning. My wife and I spin all the time, whenever our hands are free. In this way it takes two months to spin the raw cotton into yarn and another ten days to respin it after it has been dyed.
5 Two days to dye it, if you do not count all the time spent in collecting the firewood necessary to boil the dye. Then one day to make the warp. Ten days to weave, if I have time to do it continuously. Usually I have to do it on three or four separate occasions, because I have to do this and that in the village, or in Chacapampa, or in Huanuco, before finishing it. Time spent on actually
10 weaving and preparing the materials is one thing; the time elapsed from the beginning of the process to the end is another. . . .

. . . It really is a question of timing and how I can distribute my time. If the encomendero wants his cloth and wants me to serve in his house . . . during the rainy season, when I am supposed to look after my fields, then it
15 is much harder to comply. On the other hand, if he lets me assign my own work in such a way that all the tasks get evenly distributed throughout the year, then the tax burden is more manageable for me and my wife.

Peruvian Indians spinning and weaving

For instance, when we work our fields, she has to cook for all the people coming to the work party. That means that all the ingredients have to be prepared well in advance, the firewood and the helpers she needs. . . . So even if the actual plowing only takes a day or two, if I am not able to be busy those days before my field gets plowed, it is a disaster. To calculate only two days to plow is wrong, anyway, even if one would disregard the extra days of preparation. For every helper who comes to work in my field, I have to return the working day in full. And until they ask me, I have to be living in the village during the whole plowing season waiting, even though I am not actually working the whole extent of the season.

A. Answer the following questions about "Paying Tribute to the Encomendero: An Indian's Point of View" in the space provided. Do *not* look at the passage.

Peru's location in South America

1. Match each result in the left column with the correct cause in the right column.

Result

1. The man usually cannot weave for ten days continuously. _____

2. He could distribute his tasks evenly throughout the year.

Cause

a. They have helped him.

b. They must prepare to be able to feed the others.

3. He and his wife need to work *before* people begin helping them with their plowing. _____

4. He must help others with their plowing. _____

5. He has to live in the village during the whole plowing season.

_____

c. He must be available to help those who have helped him.

d. He would prefer to be responsible for distributing his own workload. _____

e. There are other things that he must do.

2. The passage is supposed to be part of an interview with an Indian who must work for the encomendero. Does it seem more like written English or spoken English to you? Why?

_____

_____

3. Whose point of view is expressed in the passage?

_____

_____

4. Write a brief summary of the passage. Write one paragraph which contains five sentences.

_____

_____

_____

_____

_____

_____

_____

_____

5. Now, write one sentence which you could use to describe the most important idea of the reading passage to someone who had not read it.

_____

_____

B. Now, reread the passage on pages 162 through 163. Then, read your partner's answers to the questions in A. Complete the following checklist.

1. Have you matched the same causes and effects in Question 1? If not, what are the differences?

_____

_____

_____

(If there are any differences, discuss them with each other and see if you can agree.)

2. Do you agree with your partner's answers to Questions 2 and 3? If not, what are the differences?

_____

_____

_____

(If there are any differences, discuss them with each other and see if you can agree.)

3. Compare the summaries that you each wrote for Question 4. Do they both contain the same information? If not, how are they different?

_____

_____

_____

4. Do the sentences that you each wrote for Question 5 contain the same information? If not, how are they different?

_____

_____

_____

After you and your partner have read each other's answers and discussed them, do you want to revise any of your answers? Use a

clean piece of paper to write your revised answers to the questions in A. Then, give your revised answers to your teacher.

Female Employment in Western Europe

Between 1975 and 1985 the number of men in the European work force fell, while the number of women rose by 9.8 million. The percentage of women working varies widely across the continent: Almost 60 percent of Danish women work compared with fewer than 30 percent of Spanish women.

5 The rise of women in the work force coincides with the growth in Europe's service sector over the past few years. Of the women in Europe who work, 73 percent are employed in the service sector, where their numbers almost equal those of men. Service-sector growth also accounts for the fact that 75 percent of newly created jobs went to women.

10 Although companies may be eager to employ them, European women are far from fully integrated into the workplace. "Women are concentrated in a restricted number of lower-paying, less prestigious occupations," says Employment in Europe, a report prepared by the European Commission's directorate general for employment, industrial relations, and social affairs. "In

15 West Germany, for example, 90 percent of women are employed in just 12 occupational groups, generally those with lower skills, despite the greater success of girls at school." An Irish Employment Equality Agency study found that in Irish electronics factories "the best-paid jobs are filled almost entirely by men and the worst-paid almost entirely by women."

20 Women also tend to work in unprotected sectors such as "outwork" and "work at home." Outwork—making crafts for tourists, for example—encompasses work at home and includes any work performed outside company premises. Such work may take place in a subcontractor's factory and is usually of the sweatshop variety. Employees are paid by the piece, though sometimes

25 a base salary is given as well. Outwork is especially prevalent in southern Europe.

Work at home is concentrated in the clothing, textile, leather goods, fur, and toy industries. In northern Europe, home work is used for metal and electrical goods manufacturing. Many firms have recruited women to work at

30 home to avoid the costs of building new factories.

Although these alternative work arrangements are widely practiced in Europe, no official statistics exist on the number of women so employed. Most of such work is paid off the books, with employees receiving no benefits of any kind, which perpetuates the impression that women are a casual part of the

35 labor force.

A. Answer the following questions about "Female Employment in Western Europe" in the space provided. Do *not* look at the passage.

1. Read each statement. If it is true according to the passage, write the letter T in the space provided. If it is false according to the passage, write the letter F in the space provided. If the passage does not contain information about the statement, write the letters NI (no information).

   a. The number of women in the European workforce increased between 1975 and 1985. _____

   b. Approximately the same percentage of women works in all European countries. _____

   c. The number of new service-related jobs in Europe has been increasing greatly. _____

   d. Many women enjoy working in service-related jobs. _____

   e. If a girl is successful at school, she can expect to get a job that pays well. _____

   f. Many women want to work at home so that they can take care of their children. _____

   g. Many companies want women to work at home because it is more economical for the companies. _____

   h. People who work at home or do outwork are usually given the same benefits as those who work in offices and factories. _____

2. Match each statement in the left column with the correct contrasting statement in the right column.

Statement	Contrasting Statement
1. Recently, the number of men in the European workforce has fallen. _____	a. Women tend to fill the worst-paid jobs.
2. European companies very much want to employ women. _____	b. A great majority of women are employed in jobs that require lower skills.
3. In West Germany, girls are generally more successful than boys at school. _____	c. There are no official statistics on the number of women doing outwork or working at home.

4. Irish men who work in electronics factories tend to hold the best-paid jobs. _____

d. At the same time, the number of women has risen.

5. Alternative work arrangements are very common in Europe. _____

e. They do not fully integrate women into the workplace.

3. Do you think that the author of the passage is neutral or sympathetic to the position of women in the Western European workforce? Why do you think so?

_____

_____

4. Write a brief summary of the passage. Write one paragraph which contains five sentences.

_____

_____

_____

_____

_____

_____

_____

_____

_____

_____

5. Now, write one sentence which you could use to describe the most important idea of the reading passage to someone who had not read it.

_____

_____

B. Now, reread the passage on page 167. Then, read your partner's answers to the questions in A. Complete the following checklist.

1. Have you marked the same statements in Question 1 as T̲, F̲, and N̲I̲? If you have not, which ones have you marked differently?

_____

(Look at the passage together and see if you can agree.)

2. Have you matched the same statements and contrasting statements in Question 2? If not, which ones have you matched differently?

_____

(Look at the passage again together and see if you can agree.)

3. Do you agree with your partner's answers to Question 3? If there are any differences, write them here.

_____

_____

_____

(If you do not agree discuss your answers and explain them to each other.)

4. Compare the summaries that you each wrote for Question 4. Do they both contain the same information? If not, how are they different?

_____

_____

_____

5. Do the sentences that you each wrote for Question 5 contain the same information? If not, how are they different?

_____

_____

_____

After you and your partner have read each other's answers and discussed them, do you want to revise any of your answers? Use a clean piece of paper to write your revised answers to the questions in A. Then, give your revised answers to your teacher.

Chinese woman at work on a farm

Chinese woman at work in a factory

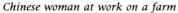

Holding up the Sky

Social, political, and economic equality of Chinese men and women has long been a central tenet of the Chinese Communist Party. There is a high number of women in the Chinese workforce—currently about 37 percent of the total. While Chinese women have prospered over the past decade, increas-
5 ing competitive pressures are eroding women's status in the workforce.

As thousands of Chinese enterprises strive to maximize profits, they are ridding their ranks of excess labor—and most of these workers are women. Generally less educated than men, Chinese women hold the redundant jobs created in years past to guarantee full employment. A survey conducted by the
10 Chinese journal *Chinese Women* indicates that about 70 percent of all employees released in job rationalization drives are female. . . .

Charges that women are more costly to employ are not totally unfounded. China's long-standing "iron rice bowl" system requires the work unit to take care of virtually all an individual's needs, [and] an employer has traditionally
15 had to pay a woman's medical bills and salary for two to three months of

maternity leave. Within the last six months or so, however, several cities have adopted new arrangements to ease the burden of maternity costs.

20   Enterprises are also encouraging female employees to modify their work habits: they are allowing (and encouraging) them to take up to seven years' maternity leave, during which they are to be paid 50–75 percent of their base salaries, and to retire at age 40 (the present age for women is 55). Although such a system may appear to give women more flexibility, recent reports indicate that many enterprises are paying only a fraction of the sum owed their female employees, some of them are not paying at all, and many of them

25   actually dismiss the women once they take their leave. Even if the factory doesn't dismiss them outright, an absence of seven years will easily render a worker obsolete and uncompetitive in a country modernizing as quickly as China. Growing ranks of women, therefore, are losing their economic independence—hardly the socialist ideal.

A. Answer the following questions about "Holding up the Sky" in the space provided. Do *not* look at the passage.

1. Choose the answer which best completes each sentence according to the passage.

   a. The Chinese Communist Party has worked actively to _____.

      (i)   encourage women to stay at home

      (ii) make women and men economically equal

      (iii) raise women's salaries

      (iv) increase the benefits paid for by employers

   b. Chinese publications _____.

      (i)   are trying to ignore the problem

      (ii) support the employers

      (iii) are publicizing the problem

      (iv) have offered constructive suggestions

   c. Benefits paid to employees are _____ most Chinese employers.

      (i)   not of great concern to

      (ii) an important part of the costs of

      (iii) paid almost equally to men and women by

      (iv) not having a great effect on the hiring of women

    d. The economic realities of China today are _____.

       (i)   encouraging women to ask for the benefits they are entitled to

       (ii)   increasing the percentage of women in the workforce

       (iii) giving women an advantage over men

       (iv) causing women to lose what they have gained

2. Write three sentences that contrast the positions of men and women in China. Describe a different contrast in each of your sentences.

    a. _____

      _____

    b. _____

      _____

    c. _____

      _____

3. Match each general statement in the left column with the correct more specific supporting statement in the right column.

General Statement

Specific Supporting Statement

1. The Chinese workforce contains a high number of women. _____

   a. About 70 percent of all employees who have lost their jobs due to "rationalization" are women.

2. Most of the excess workers that are losing their jobs in China are women. _____

   b. Women are being encouraged to take up to seven years' maternity leave.

3. A work unit has to take care of almost all of a worker's needs.

_____

   c. More than one-third of all Chinese workers are female.

4. Companies are suggesting that women modify their work habits.

_____

   d. Employers have to pay workers' medical bills.

4. Write a brief summary of the passage. Write one paragraph which contains five sentences.

_____

_____

_____

_____

_____

_____

_____

_____

_____

_____

5. Now, write one sentence which you could use to describe the most important idea of the reading passage to someone who had not read it.

_____

_____

B. Now, reread the passage on pages 171 through 172. Then, read your partner's answers to the questions in A. Complete the following checklist.

1. Do you agree with your partner's answers to Questions 1–3? If you do not agree, which answers are different?

_____

_____

_____

_____

_____

(If you do not agree discuss your answers and explain them to each other.)

2. Compare the summaries that you each wrote for Question 4. Do they both contain the same information? If not, how are they different?

_____

3. Do the sentences that you each wrote for Question 5 contain the same information? If not, how are they different?

After you and your partner have read each other's answers and discussed them, do you want to revise any of your answers? Use a clean piece of paper to write your revised answers. Then, give your revised answers to your teacher.

Women and the Labor Market: The Link Grows Stronger

Women's attachment to the labor market has increased dramatically since the end of World War II—especially for those between age 25 and 54. More than 7 of 10 women in this age group are now in the labor force, up from about 3 out of 10 four decades earlier. The rise in women's attachment to market
5   work is clearly both a product and a cause of many profound social and economic changes that have occurred in the United States over the last 40 years.

One result of this surge has been a narrowing of the gap between male and female participation rates. Also, women today display a pattern of labor
10   force participation by age group that is very different from that evident 15 years ago. Until the mid-1970's, female participation rates by age formed an "M" shape, dipping between the early twenties and the main child-bearing years of 25 to 34. That pattern has now shifted to an inverted "U" and thus is very similar to that for men. (See Chart 1.)
15   Another result is that labor market activity has become the norm for most women today. This is true for women in each 10-year group in the 25 to 54 age bracket, for whites, for blacks, and for all marital status groups. Moreover, the majority of mothers are in the labor force today—even mothers of infants and toddlers. As recently as 1975, a Bureau of Labor Statistics [BLS] study found
20   sharp differences in participation rates of women by marital status and presence and age of children. Such differences have been reduced very substantially over the ensuing decade.

Finally, women today work more hours per week and more weeks per year than they did 10 or 20 years ago. The majority of 25- to 54-year-old women
25   who worked in 1986 did so full time, year round. . . .

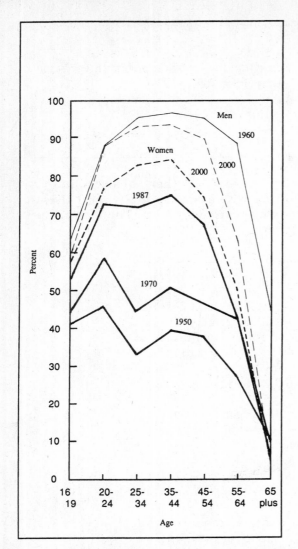

Chart 1. Civilian labor force participation rates by sex and age, selected years

Historical Trends

Women in the United States have been entering the labor market in increasing numbers over the past century, but, until the advent of the second World War, the changes were small and gradual. However, between 1940 and 1944, the number of women in the labor force jumped by 5 million—or more than

one-third. Over the same period, about 10 million men entered the Armed
Forces and, as their number in the civilian work force plummeted, women
moved in and took their places. This pattern was reversed in the following two
years. As the GI's returned home, the number of men in the civilian labor force
35   rebounded, while millions of women withdrew from the work force. However,
fewer women left at the end of World War II than had entered during the war
years, and many of those who exited in the 1944–46 period returned a few
years later. . . .

Future Outlook

40   Will women continue to enter the labor force in greater numbers? How high
will their participation rates go? How large will the proportion of women who
work year round, full time become? While there are no definite answers to
these and some other questions about women's labor market behavior in the
future, BLS recently introduced projections to the year 2000 which describe
45   some probable scenarios. The projections presume a continued increase in
female labor force participation, but at a much slower rate than during the
preceding two decades.

The primary reason for the projected slower rate of increase is that the
huge gains of the past have brought female participation rates to relatively
50   high levels. There is simply much less room to grow from a 70-percent
participation rate than there was from a 40- or 50-percent rate. . . .

While participation rates for women are expected to continue rising
through the end of the century, those for men are projected to edge further
down. As a result, the long-standing gap between male and female rates will
55   shrink even more. The following tabulation shows that the difference in the
prime working-age group, which was about 60 percentage points in 1950 (and
23 points in 1986), will narrow to 12 points by the year 2000. For 25- to 34-year
olds, the gender difference is expected to shrink to only 10 points.

	Actual, 1950		Projected 2000	
	Women	Men	Women	Men
25–54 years . . .	36.8	96.5	80.8	92.6
24–34 years . . .	34.0	96.0	82.3	93.6
35–44 years . . .	39.1	97.8	84.2	93.9
45–54 years . . .	37.9	95.8	75.4	90.1

Moreover, as the gap between male and female rates continues to narrow,
60   the outline traced by these rates over the life cycle is expected to become

increasingly unisex. In the year 2000, activity rates of women are projected to rise steadily from the teen years to a peak in the 35 to 44 age group, then to decline in the 45 to 54 age group before dropping off sharply for those 55 and over. Chart 1 notes the similarity between this pattern and that for men in the year 2000.

The shift in the outline of women's participation rates from the "M" shape to an inverted "U," which started in the 1970's, will be even more prominent by 2000. In fact, women's participation rates (in terms of both level and pattern by age) are projected to be more similar to those for men than to women's rates in 1960 or 1970. Moreover, as male rates decline over time—especially in the older age groups—the right side of their inverted "U" shifts to the left and thus becomes more like that for women.

Differences between labor market behavior of men and women shrank dramatically in the four decades following World War II. This was due largely to a tremendous increase in labor market activity by women. Over the past forty years, the proportion of 25- to 54-year-old women in the labor force jumped from one-third to more than 70 percent. Furthermore, among employed women, 3 of 4 worked full time in 1986, and well over half of them worked year round and full time. BLS projections to the year 2000 call for continued increases in market activity of women, and as a result, further convergence in male and female labor force patterns over the life cycle.

A. Answer the following questions about "Women and the Labor Market: The Link Grows Stronger" in the space provided. Do *not* look at the passage.

1. Put the following sentences in the order in which they occur in the fifth paragraph.

   a. This pattern was reversed in the following two years. _____

   b. However, between 1940 and 1944, the number of women in the labor force jumped by 5 million—or more than one-third. _____

   c. However, fewer women left at the end of World War II than had entered during the war years, and many of those who exited in the 1944–46 period returned a few years later. _____

   d. Women in the United States have been entering the labor market in increasing numbers over the past century, but, until the advent of the second World War, the changes were small and gradual. _____

e. Over the same period, about 10 million men entered the Armed Forces and, as their number in the civilian work force plummeted, women moved in and took their places. _____

f. As the GI's returned home, the number of men in the civilian labor force rebounded, while millions of women withdrew from the work force. _____

2. Read each of the following sentences from the passage. Then, in the space provided, write the type of relationship that is expressed. Choose from the following: *addition, contrast, cause and effect*.

a. One result of this surge has been a narrowing of the gap between male and female participation rates. _____

b. Moreover, the majority of mothers are in the labor force today.

_____

c. However, between 1940 and 1944, the number of women in the labor force jumped by 5 million—or more than one-third.

_____

d. While there are no definite answers to these and some other questions about women's labor market behavior in the future, BLS recently introduced projections to the year 2000 which describe some probable scenarios. _____

e. The primary reason for the projected slower rate of increase is that the huge gains of the past have brought female participation rates to relatively high levels. _____

f. Furthermore, among employed women, 3 of 4 worked full time in 1986, and well over half of them worked year round and full time.

_____

3. Write a brief summary of the passage. Write one paragraph which contains five sentences.

_____

_____

_____

_____

_____

_____

_____

_____

_____

4. Now, write one sentence which you could use to describe the most important idea of the reading passage to someone who had not read it.

_____

_____

B. Now, reread the passage on pages 175 through 178. Then, read your partner's answers to the questions in A. Complete the following checklist.

1. Do you agree with your partner's answers to Questions 1 and 2? If not, which answers are different?

_____

_____

(If you do not agree discuss your answers and explain them to each other.)

2. Compare the summaries that you each wrote for Question 3. Do they both contain the same information? If not, how are they different?

_____

_____

_____

3. Do the sentences that you each wrote for Question 4 contain the same information? If not, how are they different?

_____

_____

_____

After you and your partner have read each other's answers and discussed them, do you want to revise any of your answers? Use a clean piece of paper to write your revised answers to the questions in A. Then, give your revised answers to your teacher.

3. Looking at How It's Written

Connecting Ideas

1. Find the word or phrase that indicates the relationship in parentheses in the following passages and lines. Write the word or phrase in the space provided. The first four are done for you.

"Paying Tribute to the Encomendero: An Indian's Point of View"

    (1) <u>although</u>   (contrast)

    (15) <u>on the other hand</u> (contrast)

    (18) <u>for instance</u>   (support or example)

    (26) <u>even though</u>   (contrast)

"Female Employment in Western Europe"

    (2) _____ (contrast)

    (10) _____ (contrast)

    (16) _____ (contrast)

    (21) _____ (support or example)

    (33) _____ (support or example)

"Holding up the Sky"

    (4) _____ (contrast)

    (21) _____ (contrast)

"Women and the Labor Market: The Link Grows Stronger"

    (31) _____ (simultaneity)

    (32) _____ (simultaneity)

    (34) _____ (simultaneity)

    (42) _____ (contrast)

    (52) _____ (contrast)

    (59) _____ (simultaneity)

    (70) _____ (simultaneity)

2. Choose one or two of the passages. List some words that indicate addition and words or phrases that indicate cause and effect. Indicate the passage and the line where you have found each word or phrase.

Addition

Word or phrase	*Passage*	*Line*

Cause and Effect

Word or phrase	*Passage*	*Line*

Understanding Grammar

■ The Passive Voice

In the space provided, copy the sentences that occur in the following passages and lines. Draw a circle around the passive verb (form of the verb *to be* plus the past participle) in each sentence. (The first one is done for you.) Then answer the questions that follow.

"Paying Tribute to the Encomendero: An Indian's Point of View"

(3–4) In this way it takes two months to spin the raw cotton into yarn and another ten days to respin it after it has been dyed.

(19–20) _____
_____
_____

"Female Employment in Western Europe"

(6–8) _____

_____

_____

(28–29) _____

_____

_____

"Holding up the Sky"

(18–21) _____

_____

_____

"Women and the Labor Market: The Link Grows Stronger"

(21–22) _____

_____

_____

(33–34) _____

_____

_____

a. What part of a passive verb form changes according to its subject?

the verb *to be* _____

the past participle _____

In a passive verb form, the _____ agrees with its subject.

b. Write a corresponding sentence containing an active verb for two or three of the passive sentences.

Example (for the sentence on lines 3–4 of "Paying Tribute to the Encomendero: An Indian's Point of View"): <u>In this way it takes two months to spin the raw cotton into yarn and another ten days to respin it after we have dyed it.</u>

_____

_____

_____

_____

_____

_____

What function does the subject of a passive verb have when the verb is made active?

_____

_____

> The subject of a passive verb is the _____ in the corresponding active sentence.

Is it always possible to determine the precise subject when you change a verb from passive to active? _____

■ Reduced Adjective Clauses That Contain Present and Past Participle Adjectives

In the space provided, copy the sentences or clauses that occur in the following passages and lines. Draw a circle around the phrases that consist of a noun followed by either a present participle (-_ing_ form of the verb) or a past participle. (Two are done for you.) Then, follow the instructions given after the examples.

"Paying Tribute to the Encomendero: An Indian's Point of View"

1. (9–10) Time spent on actually weaving and preparing the materials is one thing;

2. (10–11) _____

_____

_____

3. (18–19) For instance, when we work our fields, she has to cook for all the people coming to the work party.

"Female Employment in Western Europe"

4. (2–3) _____

_____

_____

5. (11–14) _____

_____

_____

6. (21–23) _____

_____

_____

7. (32–35) _____

_____

_____

Rewrite each sentence, changing the noun followed by a present or past participle adjective to a noun followed by an adjective clause. Circle the main verb in the adjective clause and say whether it is active or passive. Two are done for you.

1. Time that is spent on actually weaving and preparing the materials is one thing; (passive)

2. _____

_____

_____

3. For instance, when we work our fields, she has to cook for all the people who [come] to the work party. (active)

4. _____

_____

_____

5. _____

_____

_____

6. _____

_____

7. _____

_____

_____

Write a rule for reducing an adjective clause that contains a passive verb.

In order to reduce an adjective clause that contains a passive verb, _____

_____

_____

Write a rule for reducing an adjective clause that contains an active verb.

In order to reduce an adjective clause that contains an active verb, _____

_____

_____

Punctuation

■ Modifying Quotations

The following version of "Holding up the Sky" differs from the one that you have read on pages 171–172. It shows how parts of the original article in *The China Business Review* have been changed.

Social, political, and economic equality of Chinese men and women . . . has long been a central tenet of the Chinese Communist Party . . . . [There is a] high number of women in the Chinese workforce—currently about . . . 37 percent of the total . . . . While Chinese women have prospered over the past decade . . . increasing competitive pressures . . . are eroding women's status in the workforce.

As thousands of Chinese enterprises strive to maximize profits, they are ridding their ranks of excess labor—and most of these workers are women. Generally less educated than men, Chinese women often hold the redundant jobs created in years past to guarantee full employment. A survey conducted by the Chinese journal *Chinese Women* indicates that about 70 percent of all employees released in job rationalization drives are female. . . .

Charges that women are more costly to employ are not totally unfounded. . . . China's long-standing "iron rice bowl" system . . . requires the work unit to take care of virtually all an individuals needs, [and] an employer has traditionally had to pay a woman's medical bills and salary for . . . two to three months of maternity leave . . . . Within the last six months or so, however, several cities have adopted new . . . arrangements to ease the burden of maternity costs . . . .

Enterprises are also encouraging female employees to modify their work habits: [they are] allowing (and encouraging) them to take up to seven years' maternity leave, during which they are to be paid 50–75 percent of their base salaries, and to retire at age 40 (the present age for women is 55). Although such a system may appear to give women more flexibility . . . , recent reports indicate that many enterprises are paying only a fraction of the sum owed their female employees, some of them are not paying at all, and many of them actually dismiss the women once they take their leave. Even if the factory doesn't dismiss them outright, an absence of seven years will easily render a worker obsolete and uncompetitive in a country modernizing as quickly as China. Growing ranks of women, therefore, are losing their economic independence— hardly the socialist ideal.

What do the uses of . . . tell you about this version of the passage compared to the original version that was published in *The China Business Review*?

_____

_____

What do the square brackets that enclose some of the words in the passage—for example [There is a] indicate?

That the enclosed words are in the original _____

That the enclosed words are *not* in the original _____

What do you think are some reasons for using these types of punctuation to show that something has been omitted from or added to the original version of a passage?

_____

_____

_____

EXERCISE: This exercise contains sentences or the beginnings of sentences that someone might use in a research paper. Use one or more parts of the sentence(s) from "Women and the Labor Market: The Link Grows Stronger" to complete the ideas of each sentence. Use quotation marks to show that you have included some of the exact words from "Women and the Labor Market: The Link Grows Stronger." Use . . . and [   ] wherever you need them. The first one is done for you.

1. There have been three results of the increase in the percentage of women working. _____

> One result of this surge has been a narrowing of the gap between male and female participation rates.
>   Another result is that labor market activity has become the norm for most women today.
>   Finally, women today work more hours per week and more weeks per year than they did 10 or 20 years ago.

There have been three results of the increase in the percentage of women working. "One . . . has been a narrowing of the gap between male and female participation rates. . . . Another . . . is that labor market activity has become the norm for most women today. . . . [The third is that] women today work more hours per week and more weeks per year than they did 10 or 20 years ago."

2. Bureau of Labor Statistics projections to the year 2000 are based on the

assumption that _____ because _____.

> While there are no definite answers to these and some other
> questions about women's labor market behavior in the future, BLS
> recently introduced projections to the year 2000 which describe some
> probable scenarios. The projections presume a continued increase in
> female labor force participation, but at a much slower rate than
> during the preceding two decades. The primary reason for the
> projected slower rate of increase is that the huge gains of the past
> have brought female participation rates to relatively high levels. There
> is simply much less room to grow from a 70-percent participation rate
> than there was from a 40- or 50-percent rate.

_____

_____

_____

_____

_____

_____

_____

_____

_____

3. The lifetime labor market participation of men and women _____

because _____.

> Moreover, as the gap between male and female rates continues to
> narrow, the outline traced by these rates over the life cycle is
> expected to become increasingly unisex. In the year 2000, activity
> rates of women are projected to rise steadily from the teen years to a
> peak in the 35 to 44 age group, then to decline in the 45 to 54 age
> group before dropping off sharply for those 55 and over.

_____

_____

_____

_____

_____

_____

_____

_____

_____

_____

Now, choose some quotations from some of the passages that you have read for your research. Write sentences that contain some but not all of the words from the quotations. Use quotation marks, . . . , and [   ] as you need them.

4. *Original Quotation:*

_____

_____

_____

_____

_____

Incorporated Quotation:

_____

_____

_____

_____

_____

5. *Original Quotation:*

_____

_____

_____

_____

Incorporated Quotation:

_____

_____

_____

_____

_____

6. *Original Quotation:*

_____

_____

_____

_____

_____

Incorporated Quotation:

_____

_____

_____

_____

_____

■ Using Dashes

EXERCISE: Find the sentences that contain dashes (—) on the given lines of each reading passage. Copy each sentence in the space provided. Then, rewrite the sentence without the dash(es) or the material between or after them. (The first one is done for you.) Then answer the questions that follow.

"Female Employment in Western Europe":

(21–23): <u>Outwork—making crafts for tourists, for example—encompasses work at home and includes any work performed outside company premises.</u>
    <u>Outwork encompasses work at home and includes any work performed outside company premises.</u>

"Holding up the Sky":

2–4: _____

_____

_____

_____

6–7: _____

_____

_____

_____

28–29: _____

_____

_____

_____

"Women and the Labor Market: The Link Grows Stronger"

1–2: _____

_____

_____

_____

17–19: _____

_____

_____

_____

29–31: _____

_____

_____

_____

70–72: _____

_____

_____

_____

1. Is the material that comes between or after the dashes necessary to the basic meaning of the sentence?

     yes _____   no _____

2. When the dashes and the material that comes between or after them are omitted, is the sentence grammatical?

     yes _____   no _____

3. What kind of information is put between dashes or after one dash?

     _____

     _____

4. What effect does putting information between dashes or after one dash have on the reader's evaluation of it?

     _____

     _____

5. How frequently are dashes used in the reading passages in this chapter?

     _____

EXERCISE: **Combine each pair of sentences, using one or two dashes. The first one is done for you.**

1. A lot of families are having to choose between making enough money and raising their children well. This is not a good choice from society's point of view.

     A lot of families are having to choose between making enough money and raising their children well—not a good choice from society's point of view.

2. More and more American women with children under the age of three are in the labor force. In 1987, the percentage was 55.2.

     _____

     _____

     _____

3. This means that more than five out of ten women with infants or toddlers are in the labor force. More than five out of ten is more than half.

     _____

     _____

     _____

4. Fathers can also stay home and take care of their children. This is an idea that some families are trying.

_____

_____

_____

4. PREPARING TO WRITE

Understanding Why

■ Oral and Written Styles

Reread "Paying Tribute to the Encomendero: An Indian's Point of View." Does it seem like a written passage, or does it seem like the written form of what someone has said?

written passage _____

written form of what someone has said _____

How can you tell?

_____

_____

■ Looking at the Author's Intention

Discuss at least two of the four passages in this chapter with your partner or group. What was the most interesting thing about each of them? Write your ideas in the space provided.

_____

_____

_____

_____

_____

_____

_____

Which of the passages did you find the most interesting? Why? Was that the passage that you expected to be the most interesting? Write your answers in the space provided.

_____
_____
_____
_____
_____
_____
_____
_____
_____

Looking at Organization

■ Thesis Statements

With your partner or group, find the thesis statements in each of the last three readings and write them in the space provided. Tell where you found the thesis statement (paragraph and lines).

"Female Employment in Western Europe":

_____
_____
_____

(lines _____, paragraph _____)

"Holding up the Sky":

_____
_____
_____

(lines _____, paragraph _____)

"Women and the Labor Market: The Link Grows Stronger":

_____

_____

_____

(lines _____, paragraph _____)

■ Outlining to Show Function, Topic, and Method of Support

Study the outline with your partner or group. Then, choose either "Holding up the Sky" or "Women and the Labor Market" to outline together. (As in the example, if there is no topic sentence in a particular paragraph, try to write one.) Write your outline on a clean piece of paper and give it to your teacher.

Paragraph Outline of "Female Employment in Western Europe"

(I) *Function:* This paragraph is an introduction to the passage.

Topic Sentence: The number of women in the European work force has increased and varies from country to country. (The paragraph does not actually contain a topic sentence.)

Method of Support: statistics and specific examples

(II) *Function:* This paragraph gives one possible reason for the increase in the number of women in the European work force.

Topic Sentence: The rise of women in the workforce coincides with the growth in Europe's service sector over the past few years. (lines 5–6)

Method of Support: statistics

(III) *Function:* This paragraph contrasts the high number of women in the European work force with their lack of integration into the workplace. It contains the **thesis statement** of the passage.

Topic Sentence: Women are concentrated in a restricted number of lower-paying, less prestigious occupations. (lines 11–12)

Method of Support: statistics and statements by authorities

(IV) *Function:* This paragraph describes another way in which European women are not integrated into the workplace.

Topic Sentence: Women also tend to work in unprotected sectors such as "outwork" and "work at home." (lines 20–21)

Method of Support: description of an example

(V) *Function:* This paragraph further describes a type of work that women tend to do.

Topic Sentence: Work at home is used in certain industries in order to lower costs. (The paragraph does not actually contain a topic sentence.)

Method of Support: examples

(VI) *Function:* This paragraph is the conclusion to the passage and gives a result of women's lack of integration into the work force.

Topic Sentence: No official statistics exist on the number of women so employed. (line 32)

Method of Support: reason (Most of such work is paid off the books.)

■ Different Types of Introductory Paragraphs

Reread the introductory paragraph of each of the last three passages. Decide which one fits each of the descriptions and write its title in the space provided.

This introductory paragraph contrasts the present situation with the recent past.

_____

_____

This introductory paragraph gives a brief historical overview of its topic and then mentions causal relationships.

_____

_____

This introductory paragraph describes recent trends.

_____

_____

How many of these three introductory paragraphs end in the thesis sentence of the entire passage? _____

■ Different Types of Concluding Paragraphs

Reread the concluding paragraph of each of the last three passages. Decide which one fits each of the descriptions and write its title in the space provided.

This concluding paragraph restates and expands on the thesis statement of the passage.

_____

_____

This concluding paragraph summarizes the trends described in the passage.

_____

_____

This concluding paragraph gives a detailed description of one result of what has been discussed.

_____

_____

Applying What You Have Studied

■ Putting Ideas Together

Choosing a Tentative Thesis Statement   By now, you have done some research on the topic that you chose in Chapter 4. Although you will continue to get information, you probably have an idea of what you want to write about. Based on this idea, you can write a tentative thesis statement, which will help to guide you in your future research.

> Your thesis statement will control the type of information that you put into your paper.

Talk with your partner about each other's topics and research. Tell your partner the point of view that you want to express in your paper, and listen to the point of view that your partner wants to express. Spend ten minutes writing possible thesis statements. Then, discuss your statements with each other. You may then choose the one that you think best expresses what you want to write about. You may also decide to write a different thesis statement.

Possible Thesis Statements for My Paper

_____

_____

_____

_____

_____

_____

_____

_____

_____

_____

Writing a Tentative Outline   Write your thesis statement in the space provided. Based on your research and your tentative thesis statement, write a tentative outline for your paper in the space provided. In your outline, indicate a topic sentence for each paragraph (although you may not actually write the sentence in your paragraph later). Also say what type of support you will provide for your topic sentence. If it is possible for you to do so now, you may also describe the function of each paragraph in your paper.

Show your outline to your partner, and look at your partner's outline. Make suggestions for changes or additions to each other. Then, revise your outlines and give them to your teacher. Remember that, like your thesis statement, your outline will guide the direction that your research takes. However, you can modify both of them if your continuing research changes your ideas about your topic.

Tentative Thesis Statement

_____

_____

_____

Tentative Outline

_____

_____

_____

_____

_____

_____

_____

_____

_____

_____

_____

_____

_____

Planning and Doing Research   Meet with your partner or group. Discuss your tentative thesis statements and outlines with each other. Answer questions about the information that you have already gotten from your research. Make suggestions about what other information each of you needs to complete your papers. Also, make suggestions about what kinds of sources each of you can use to find this information.

Suggestions about Information That I Need to Complete My Paper

_____

_____

_____

_____

_____

_____

_____

_____

_____

_____

_____

Suggestions about Sources That I Can Consult for Information

_____

_____

_____

_____

_____

_____

_____

_____

_____

_____

_____

■ Expanding Your Ideas

Displaying Information in Tables and Graphs

EXERCISE: Look at the table in "Women and the Labor Market: The Link Grows Stronger" on page 177. Then, answer these questions.

1. About how many words or sentences would you need to give all of the information that is presented in the table?

   _____

2. How long do you think it would take most people to understand the information if it were presented in sentences?

   _____

3. Is it easier to process the information the way it is presented or in sentence form?

   _____

4. The following graphs present the same information as in the table. Which method of presenting this specific information do you find clearer: the table, the bar graph, or the pie graphs?

   table _____   bar graph _____   pie graph _____

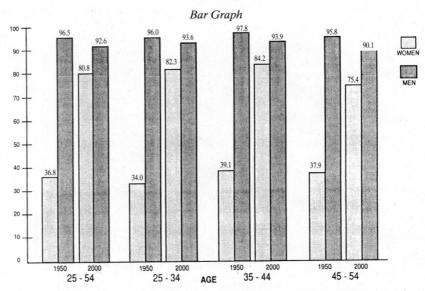

Percentage of Men & Women in U.S. Labor Force by age—1950 and 2000 (projected)

Pie Graph

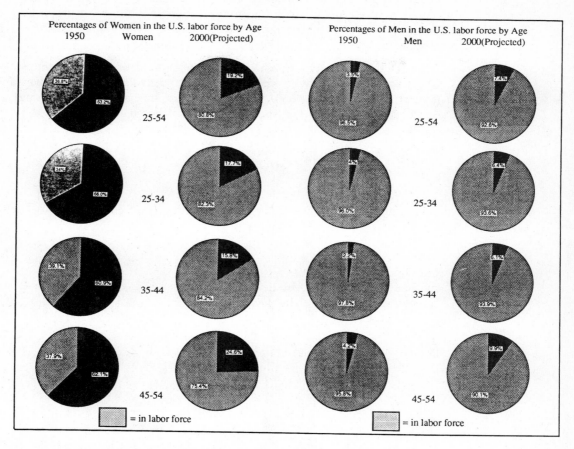

Percentages of Women in the U.S. labor force by Age
1950   Women   2000(Projected)

Percentages of Men in the U.S. labor force by Age
1950   Men   2000(Projected)

25-54

25-34

35-44

45-54

☐ = in labor force   ☐ = in labor force

Percentage of men and women in U.S. labor force by age—1950 and 2000 (projected)

5. Use the space provided to describe some of the advantages of the table, some of the bar graph, and some of the pie graph.

_____

_____

_____

_____

_____

_____

_____

EXERCISE: With your partner choose one or more of the following sets of information. Present the given information using a table, a bar graph, or a pie graph. Then, use the space provided to explain why you chose that particular method of presentation for this information.

1. In the United States, in March 1987, the percentage of different groups of women aged 25 to 54 who were working in the civilian labor force was as follows: never married/81.5%; married with the husband living at home/ 68.1%; married with the husband not living at home/70.9%; widowed/ 65.7%; divorced/84.7%.

   Presentation:

   Reasons for choosing to present this information using a _____

   _____

   _____

   _____

2. The following were the rates of civilian labor force participation for American women aged 25 to 54 according to race for the specified years. 1954: White/37.0%; Nonwhite*/53.4%. 1967: White/45.7%; Nonwhite/59.3%. 1977: White/57.7%; Nonwhite/63.7%; Black/64.4%. 1987: White/71.8%; Nonwhite/72.1%; Black/73.6%. (*Nonwhite includes black.)

Presentation:

Reasons for choosing to present this information using a _____

_____

_____

_____

3. In the United States, the percentage of women aged 25 to 54 in each marital category was as follows for each year. Never married: 1957/7.5%; 1987/12.9%. Married with the husband living at home: 1957/80.5%; 1987/68.2%. Married with the husband not living at home: 1957/4.3%; 1987/4.9%. Widowed: 1957/4.6%; 1987/2.2%. Divorced: 1957/3.0%; 1987/ 11.8%.

Presentation:

Reasons for choosing to present this information using a _____

_____

_____

_____

EXERCISE: Choose one or two sets of figures from the research that you are doing. Present the information using whichever method you think is best: a table, a bar graph, or a pie graph.

Trying out Different Introductions   Write at least two different tentative introductions to your paper. Let your partner read them, and read the introductions that your partner has written. Discuss them with each other. Say which one you like best and why. Write down your partner's comments, or ask him or her to write them for you. (If your partner asks you to, write down your comments.) Save them and think about them. Don't make a decision about your introduction yet.

Trying out Different Conclusions   Write at least two different tentative conclusions to your paper. Let your partner read them, and read the conclusions that your partner has written. Discuss them with each other. Say which one you like best and why. Write down your partner's comments, or ask him or her to write them for you. (If your partner asks you to, write down your comments.) Save them and think about them. Don't make a decision about your conclusion yet. You will make a tentative decision later in this chapter, but you should also realize that as you continue to do research your ideas about your conclusion may change.

Continuing Your Research   Review what you wrote on page 201. Decide what further research you need to do. Write a list for yourself in the space provided.

Further Research That I Need to Do

_____

_____

_____

_____

Begin to do your further research as soon as possible. You should spend at least some of each school day for the next week (or whatever period of time your teacher tells you to use) on the research that you need to do.

5. WRITING MORE

In this chapter, you have written or created the following tentative parts of your research paper:

Thesis statement (page 200)
Outline (page 200)
Tables or graphs (page 200)
Introductions
Conclusions

Reread each part and modify it according to your additional research or any other reasons you may have for changing it.

6. WRITING IT RIGHT

Study the parts of the Portfolio of Grammatical Forms, Usage, and Exercises on pages 309–320 that your teacher tells you to study. Proofread the thesis statement, introductions, and conclusions that your partner has chosen. Then, complete this section in your partner's book.

1. If there are quotations, are . . . and [   ] used correctly and as needed? (Review pages 187–191.)
   Use this space to write any sentences that you think need to be changed.

   _____

   _____

   _____

2. If there are connectors that show contrast, simultaneity, or support, are they used correctly? (Review page 180.)
   Use this space to write any sentences that you think need to be changed.

   _____

   _____

   _____

   Use this space to indicate any places where you think that connectors that show contrast, simultaneity, or support could be added.

   _____

   _____

3. If there are sentences containing dashes, are they punctuated correctly? (Review pages 191–194.)
   Use this space to write any sentences that you think need to be changed.

   _____

   _____

   _____

4. Are there any sentences that contain passive voice verbs? Are they correct? (Review pages 182–184.)
   Use this space to write any sentences that you think need to be changed.

   _____

   _____

   _____

   Use this space to indicate any places where you think that the passive voice could be used.

   _____

   _____

5. Are there any sentences that contain present or past participle adjectives? Are they used correctly? (Review pages 184–186.)
   Use this space to write any sentences that you think need to be changed.

   _____

   _____

   _____

   Use this space to indicate any places where you think that present or past participle adjectives could be used.

   _____

   _____

Return your partner's tentative thesis statement, introduction, and conclusion, and take back yours. Study your partner's proofreading, and ask any questions that you may have.

7. WRITING IT OVER

Reread the thesis statement, introductions, and conclusions drafts that you have proofread for your partner. Also look at the tentative outline and any tables or graphs. Complete this section in each other's books. (Put your name in the blank.)

_____'s *Comments and Suggestions about My Research Paper*

1. I look forward to reading your research paper because _____

   _____

   _____

2. I like your tentative thesis statement because _____

   _____

   _____

3. Please consider changing your thesis statement in the following way:

   _____

   _____

4. It would be a good idea if you changed your tentative outline in the following ways:

   _____

   _____

5. You could make your tables or graphs clearer if you _____

   _____

   _____

6. The introduction that I prefer is the one that begins:

   _____

   I like it the best because _____

   _____

7. The conclusion that I prefer is the one that begins:

   _____

I like it the best because _____

_____

Think over your partner's comments and suggestions. Remember, the final decisions are yours. Revise any part of your paper that you want to, and write or draw it on a clean piece of paper. Give these to your teacher.

8. MORE RESEARCH

Make another copy of your tentative outline of your paper. Skip lines and use wide margins for this copy. In the margins or between the lines that you have written on, note which sources you have used for each piece of information. Wherever you realize that you will need more information, write the phrase *more information needed* in a different color.

Read your partner's outline and comments, and let your partner read yours. Tell each other if you think that you need more information, or if you need to give credit to more sources. Then, modify your outline and comments. Finally, copy your modified annotated outline onto a clean piece of paper and give it to your teacher.

After your teacher returns your outline, make a list of all of the information that you still need. Try to spend at least some time every school day doing more research to get this information. Be sure that you write down all of the information you need about the source from which you get your information.

9. PERSONAL GLOSSARY

Use the space provided to write any other words that you learned in this chapter. Also, write a definition for each word.

_____

_____

_____

_____

_____

_____

_____

_____

_____

_____

_____

_____

_____

_____

_____

_____

_____

_____

_____

_____

_____

_____

_____

_____

_____

_____

_____

_____

6 Families and Roles

Rhetorical focus: writing definitions; emphasis and position in a paragraph; connectors that show different relationships

Organizational focus: topic sentences and paragraph organization; thesis statement and organization

Grammatical focus: unreal conditionals

Mechanical focus: giving credit for information and ideas; avoiding plagiarism; proper bibliographic form; putting citations within the text of a paper

A United States nuclear family in the 1950s

A family in Jakarta, Java

A Hispanic-American family

A traditional Japanese wedding

1. THINKING ABOUT IT

Talk with your partner. Tell each other about your families.

How many people are there in your family?

Do all of them live together?

Who works outside the home?

Is there a difference between the roles of men and women?

Do people have different roles depending on their ages?

What about families in other cultures that you know about?

Are they the same as families in your culture, or are they different?

What about your family and your partner's?

How are they the same?

How are they different?

Do you think that one form of family is better than another? Why (not)?

Use the space provided to write a brief definition of an ideal family. When you are finished, exchange definitions with your partner. Discuss your definitions with each other.

An Ideal Family

_____

_____

_____

_____

_____

_____

_____

_____

_____

_____

2. READING AND REMEMBERING

There are four readings in this section. The first is a short definition of the family. It is taken from a book titled *Social Structure*, by George Peter Murdock. This passage is the first paragraph of the first chapter of the book, called "The Nuclear Family." (A nuclear family consists of a father, a mother, and their children.)

The second reading—"Should Men and Women Have Different Roles?"—comes from a book by the famous anthropologist Margaret Mead. The book is called *Sex and Temperament in Three Primitive Societies*. This passage comes from the conclusion of the book.

The third reading is taken from an article in a book entitled *Family, Household and Gender Relations in Latin America*, edited by Elizabeth Jelin. The article, called "Dynastic Growth and Survival Strategies," was written by Larissa A. Lomnitz and Marisol Perez-Lizaur. It describes some changes that have taken place in a Mexican grand (extended) family, the Gomez family, that began in the late nineteenth century.

The final reading is about Korean families and their values. It comes from a book called *New Urban Immigrants: The Korean*

Community in New York, **by Illsoo Kim. The passage is taken from Chapter 10, entitled "The Origin of the Character Structure of Korean Immigrants." In the passage, Dr. Kim discusses the influence of Confucianism on the Korean family.**

Your teacher will tell you which reading(s) to do. After you complete a reading, answer the questions which follow it. When you have finished with the reading(s), answer the questions on page 226 if your teacher tells you to.

The Family

The family is a social group characterized by common residence, economic cooperation, and reproduction. It includes adults of both sexes, at least two of whom maintain a socially approved sexual relationship, and one or more children, own or adopted, of the sexually cohabiting adults. The family is to
5 be distinguished from marriage, which is a complex of customs centering upon the relationship between a sexually associating pair of adults within the family. Marriage defines the manner of establishing and terminating such a relationship, the normative behavior and reciprocal obligations within it, and the locally accepted restrictions upon its personnel.

A. Answer the following questions about "The Family" in the space provided. Do *not* look at the passage.

1. What is the minimum number of adults in a family?

   _____

2. What is the minimum number of children?

   _____

3. Are marriage and the family the same or different?

   _____

4. Write a definition of the family in your own words.

   _____

   _____

   _____

   _____

5. Based on this definition, can we expect different cultures to have different kinds of families?

yes ———   no ———

B. Now, reread the passage on page 215. Then, read your partner's answers to the questions in A. Complete the following checklist.

1. Do you agree with your partner's answers to Questions 1, 2, 3, and 5? If you do not agree, what are the differences?

———————————————————————————

———————————————————————————

———————————————————————————

Discuss your answers and explain them to each other.

2. Compare the definitions that you each wrote for Question 4. Do they both contain the same information? If not, how are they different?

———————————————————————————

———————————————————————————

———————————————————————————

3. Do they contain the same information as the original passage? If not, how are they different?

———————————————————————————

———————————————————————————

———————————————————————————

After you and your partner have read each other's answers and discussed them, do you want to revise any of your answers? Use a clean piece of paper to write your revised answers to the questions in A. Then, give your revised answers to your teacher.

Should Men and Women Have Different Roles?

There are at least three courses open to a society that has realized the extent to which male and female personality are socially produced. Two of these courses have been tried before, over and over again, at different times in the long, irregular, repetitive history of the race. The first is to standardize the personality of men and women as clearly contrasting, complementary, and
5   antithetical . . . .

Such a system would be wasteful of the gifts of many women who could exercise other functions far better than their ability to bear children in an already overpopulated world. It would be wasteful of the gifts of many men
10 who could exercise their special personality gifts far better in the home than in the market-place. It would be wasteful, but it would be clear. It could attempt to guarantee to each individual the role for which society insisted upon training him or her, and such a system would penalize only those individuals who, in spite of all the training, did not display the approved
15 personalities. . . .

Alternatively, society can take the course that has become especially associated with the plans of most radical groups: admit that men and women are capable of being moulded to a single pattern as easily as to a diverse one, and cease to make any distinction in the approved personality of both sexes.
20 . . .

In evaluating such a programme as this, however, it is necessary to keep in mind the nature of the gains that society has achieved in its most complex forms. A sacrifice of distinctions in sex-personality may mean a sacrifice in complexity. . . .

25 However, the only solution of the problem does not lie between an acceptance of standardization of sex-differences with the resulting cost in individual happiness and adjustment, and the abolition of these differences with the consequent loss in social values. A civilization might take its cues not from such categories as age or sex, race or hereditary position in a family line,
30 but instead of specializing personality along such simple lines recognize, train, and make a place for many and divergent temperamental endowments. It might build upon the different potentialities that it now attempts to extirpate artifically in some children and create artificially in others. . . .

Historically our own culture has relied for the creation of rich and
35 contrasting values upon many artificial distinctions, the most striking of which is sex. It will not be by the mere abolition of these distinctions that society will develop patterns in which individual gifts are given place instead of being forced into an ill-fitting mould. If we are to achieve a richer culture, rich in contrasting values, we must recognize the whole gamut of human
40 potentialities, and so weave a less arbitrary social fabric, one in which each diverse human gift will find a fitting place.

A. Answer the following questions about "Should Men and Women Have Different Roles?" in the space provided. Do *not* look at the passage.

1. According to the passage, are the personalities of men and women determined by their sex or by their society?

_____

2. How many different courses can a society take to deal with this?

   _____

3. What are they?

   _____

   _____

   _____

4. Which of these has been tried "over and over again"?

   _____

   _____

5. Which does the author of the passage, Margaret Mead, believe is the best?

   _____

6. Write one paragraph in which you summarize the most important ideas of the passage.

   _____

   _____

   _____

   _____

   _____

   _____

   _____

   _____

   _____

   _____

7. Now, write one sentence which you could use to describe the most important idea of the passage to someone who had not read it.

   _____

   _____

B. Now, reread the passage on pages 216 through 217. Then, read your partner's answers to the questions in A. Complete the following checklist.

1. Do you agree with your partner's answers to Questions 1–5? If you do not agree, what are the differences?

_____

_____

_____

_____

Discuss your answers and explain them to each other.

2. Compare the summaries that you wrote in Question 6 and the sentence that you wrote in Question 7. Do they both contain the same information? If not, how are they different?

_____

_____

_____

3. Do they contain the same information as the original passage? If not, how are they different?

_____

_____

_____

After you and your partner have read each other's answers and discussed them, do you want to revise any of your answers? Use a clean piece of paper to write your revised answers to the questions in A. Then, give your revised answers to your teacher.

The Later Development of a Mexican Grand Family

Leopoldo's sons . . . started to form their own branches, choosing to buy lots and houses in various neighbourhoods. As their offspring married, they received a piece of land close to their parents' to build their own houses. The result shows up in the prevalence of three-generational residential com-
5 pounds: grandparents, sons or daughters, and grandchildren living in a restricted area of the city, with very frequent interaction among themselves. Cousins play together continuously and grow up as if they were siblings. Some domestic functions are shared by relatives, especially rituals.

As the older generations died, the social relations between the various
10 branches became more distant, being limited to compulsory attendance at
funerals or invitations to christenings and weddings, and the economic differences more relevant. Contacts were renewed and information exchanged on the
occasions of such gatherings, but the family had grown to nearly unmanageable
proportions, making it impossible to keep contact with the whole network.

15 In between major social occasions, face-to-face relations have been largely
replaced by telephone contact. In each branch information is centralized and
transmitted by certain female figures who may be called centralizing women.
These self-appointed keepers of the family tradition appear to fulfill an
important role in channelling, switching and storing information that per-
20 tains to the entire kinship network.

There is a strict separation between male and female roles. A male
member of the family wishes ideally to be his own boss, that is, to become an
independent businessman/entrepreneur. In the context of family ideology, it
is unseemly for a man to work for an outsider, and particularly for the
25 government. Those unable to stand on their own feet would be given employment in a family business. Thus, an entrepreneur expects his sons to follow in
his footsteps, to work from an early age under his direct supervision, and to
take over a preassigned share of his business interests at his death.

This hard-headed competitive ideology was tempered by a strong feeling of
30 noblesse oblige towards relatives, in order of social closeness. The elderly, widows,
spinsters and other relatives in need were not to be allowed to seek charity outside
the family bounds. This feeling of responsibility often extended to faithful
servants and employees: after they had been with the entrepreneur for a long
time, they would be treated like poor relatives. Women frequently provided the
35 basic information which enabled the family entrepreneurs to channel resources
to relatives in trouble. The typical centralizing woman was forever organizing
parties and get-togethers of every description; she was a living calendar of
birthdays, saint's days and other memorabilia. She also kept wayward relatives in line through solicited or unsolicited advice. . . .

40 The economic pattern of the most recent generations reflects the economic
evolution of Mexico. Today the sons of big entrepreneurs are sent to college to
obtain a degree in business administration and later given a chance to enter
business at a suitable management level; not so other relatives. The 'family
business' pattern subsists only in the smaller, traditional and technologically
45 backward enterprises. Family ideology survives in the form of mutual assistance among relatives. Family affiliation alone is no longer sufficient to assure
a comfortable living; the resources afforded by reciprocal aid, which exists
potentially in the kinship network, have to be cultivated through conscious
effort. Family pride, solidarity and tradition remain as important as ever, but
50 the rugged individualism and anti-political bias of previous generations have
been tempered by an acceptance of the new realities of Mexican economic life.

A. Answer the following questions about "The Later Development of a Mexican Grand Family" in the space provided. Do *not* look at the passage.

1. Put these sentences order. Then, check the passage to see if your answers are correct.

   a. As the older generations died, the social relations between the various branches became more distant, being limited to compulsory attendance at funerals or invitations to christenings and weddings, and the economic differences more relevant. _____

   b. The economic pattern of the most recent generations reflects the economic evolution of Mexico. _____

   c. Leopoldo's sons . . . started to form their own branches, choosing to buy lots and houses in various neighbourhoods. _____

   d. In between major social occasions, face-to face relations have been largely replaced by telephone contact. _____

2. In the Gomez family, are male and female roles the same or different?

   _____

3. What are centralizing women?

   _____

   _____

4. What are some of the changes that have taken place in the Gomez family?

   _____

   _____

   _____

   _____

5. Write a brief summary of the passage.

   _____

   _____

   _____

   _____

   _____

_____

_____

_____

_____

_____

6. Now, write one sentence which you could use to describe the most important idea of the reading passage to someone who had not read it.

_____

_____

B. Now, reread the passage on pages 219 through 220. Then, read your partner's answers to the questions in A. Complete the following checklist.

1. Do you agree with your partner's answers to Questions 1–4? If you do not agree, what are the differences?

_____

_____

_____

Discuss your answers and explain them to each other.

2. Compare the summaries that you wrote in Question 5 and the sentence that you wrote in Question 6. Do they both contain the same information? If not, how are they different?

_____

_____

_____

3. Do they contain the same information as the original passage? If not, how are they different?

_____

_____

_____

After you and your partner have read each other's answers and discussed them, do you want to revise any of your answers? Use a

clean piece of paper to write your revised answers to the questions in A. Then, give your revised answers to your teacher.

The Influence of Confucianism on Korean Families

Confucian values and norms . . . imposed an indelible stamp on the institution of the Korean family, for they governed both intra- and interfamily relationships.

5 Within the family household an individual's status depended on his generation, relative age, and sex. Generation was the primary factor, and grandparents and parents of either sex had to be treated with considerable respect by their descendants. Within a generation, however, sex and age were the determinants; a wife was inferior to her husband, a sister to her brother, and a younger brother to his older brother. Within 10 a larger societal context, an individual's status was in part related to his age but was also greatly related to the status of his family in society, whether noble or common, a family of scholars or of peasants. Family status also depended on the number of generations of ancestors whose memorial tablets were kept and honored.*

15 Largely from the influence of this Confucian past, Koreans still closely attach themselves to the family. Its preservation and propagation still constitutes a paramount social norm, and loyalties and obligations toward the family supersede all others. In order to ensure the continuation of the past in the present through the family, traditional Koreans systematically worshiped 20 their ancestors. This ancestral worship still continues among contemporary urban Koreans. . . . Furthermore, an individual is still defined and evaluated as a part of the family. One's success is construed as a success for the family; one's failure is counted as a family failure. Koreans still scold their own family members by saying that "you are a shame to our family," or "you are a cause 25 of disgrace to our family."

Nonetheless, the Korean family has undergone tremendous change in the rapid urbanization, industrialization, and modernization of South Korea. The nuclear family has begun to replace the three-generation extended family, the ideal traditional Confucian family form. Large-scale social institutions have 30 begun to take over the original functions of the Korean family. Centers for the elderly and nursing homes have come into being, and gerontology has recently been accepted as a field of social science. And parental authority has declined. . . .

*Vreeland et al., *Arca Handbook,* p. 85.

In spite of these recent changes, the institution of the family is still a primordial social force in South Korean society. According to a recent survey,
35 41.1 percent of Korean householders spend the largest portion of their income on the education of their children. In the new land [the United States], this family-centered success ethic has greatly facilitated upward mobility. . . . Korean success in labor-intensive small businesses presupposes the willingness of all family members. As a result, many Korean small businessmen in
40 New York City are able to send their children to Ivy League schools. A Korean greengrocer said, with pride, "My son comes here every weekend from Princeton to help me." And of course Korean parents with school-age children worry about inner-city schools, saying that "we have to move to the suburbs for the education of our children."

A. Answer the following questions about "The Influence of Confucianism on Korean Families" in the space provided. Do *not* look at the passage.

1. What three factors influenced an individual's status within the family?

2. Which of these was the most important?

3. According to the passage, what is the most important institution to Koreans?

4. What has caused changes in the traditional Korean family?

5. According to the passage, what one factor has made upward mobility possible for Koreans in the United States?

6. Write a brief summary of the passage.

_____

_____

_____

_____

_____

_____

7. Now, write one sentence which you could use to describe the most important idea of the reading passage to someone who had not read it.

_____

_____

B. Now, reread the passage on pages 223 through 224. Then, read your partner's answers to the questions in A. Complete the following checklist.

1. Do you agree with your partner's answers to Questions 1–5? If you do not agree, what are the differences?

_____

_____

_____

_____

Discuss your answers and explain them to each other.

2. Compare the summaries that you wrote in Question 6 and the sentence that you wrote in Question 7. Do they both contain the same information? If not, how are they different?

_____

_____

_____

3. Do they contain the same information as the original passage? If not, how are they different?

_____

_____

_____

After you and your partner have read each other's answers and discussed them, do you want to revise any of your answers? Use a clean piece of paper to write your revised answers to the questions in A. Then, give your revised answers to your teacher.

Comparing and Contrasting the Information and Opinions in the Four Passages

A. Answer the following questions based on your understanding of the four reading passages and the information that you have gotten from your partner and other classmates.

Passage A: "The Family"

Passage B: "Should Men and Women Have Different Roles?"

Passage C: "The Later Development of a Mexican Grand Family"

Passage D: "The Influence of Confucianism on Korean Families"

1. Do the Mexican and Korean families that are described in Passages C and D fit the definition of the family given in Passage A?

   yes _____   no _____   Why (not)?

   _____

   _____

   _____

   _____

2. Which course of action as defined in Passage B has been followed by the Mexican and Korean societies described in Passages C and D?

   _____

3. Overall, are the types of families described in Passages C and D more similar to each other or more different from each other?

   more similar _____   more different _____ Explain your answer.

   _____

   _____

   _____

   _____

B. Read your partner's answers to the questions in A. Do you agree with them? If you do not agree discuss your answers and explain them to each other.

After you and your partner have read each other's answers and discussed them, do you want to revise any of your answers? Use a clean piece of paper to write your revised answers to the questions in A. Then, give your revised answers to your teacher.

3. LOOKING AT HOW IT'S WRITTEN

Connecting Ideas

1. Find the sentences in the following lines that contain each connector. Copy each sentence and the one that comes before it in the space provided.

   "Should Men and Women Have Different Roles?"

   16–19 (*alternatively*) _____

   _____

   _____

   _____

   "The Later Development of a Mexican Grand Family"

   26–28 (*thus*) _____

   _____

   _____

   _____

   "The Influence of Confucianism on Korean Families"

   21–22 (*furthermore*) _____

   _____

   _____

   _____

   26–27 (*nonetheless*) _____

   _____

_____

_____

34–35 (*in spite of*) _____

_____

_____

_____

39–40 (*as a result*) _____

_____

_____

_____

2. Put each connector from Question 1 in the appropriate list according to the relationship it indicates. Other connectors that show these relationships begin each list.

Connectors That Show Different Relationships		
Addition	Contrast	Cause and Effect
and	but	because; so
moreover	however	therefore
_____	_____	_____
_____	_____	_____
_____	_____	_____
_____	_____	_____

3. Underline the sentences that contain *such* in the following lines. Then, draw a circle around the nouns or phrases that each phrase containing *such* refers to. If you cannot find a referent, write one in the margin.

"The Family": lines 7–9

"Should Men and Women Have Different Roles?": lines 7–9; 11–15; 21–23; 28–31

"The Later Development of a Mexican Grand Family": lines 12–15

Understanding Grammar

◾ Unreal or Hypothetical Conditionals

1. Reread the second paragraph of "Should Men and Women Have Different Roles?" Underline the verb forms that contain *could* or *would*. What meaning do these forms express?

    habitual action in the past _____

    unreal or hypothetical conditions _____

    preference _____

2. What does *unreal* mean? (Use your dictionary or ask your teacher if you don't know.)

    _____

    What does *hypothetical* mean? (Use your dictionary or ask your teacher if you don't know.)

    _____

3. Margaret Mead, the author of the passage, says that societies such as the one she describes in the second paragraph have existed throughout human history. What does she presuppose in using **unreal conditional** forms to talk about such a society?

    She knows that it doesn't exist. _____

    She thinks that it should not exist. _____

    She is imagining such a society, not talking about a particular one that really exists. _____

4. The following sentence occurs on line 7 of "The Later Development of a Mexican Grand Family":

    Cousins play together continuously and grow up as if they were siblings.

    According to the sentence, is it true or not true that the cousins are siblings?

    true _____   not true _____

    Which verb shows this? _____

4. PREPARING TO WRITE

Understanding Why

■ Looking at the Author's Intention

Your teacher will tell you which of these sections to do and whether to report your answers to your partner, your group, or the whole class.

A. "The Family"

1. What is the main purpose of the passage?

   _____

2. Why does the author write about marriage if his purpose is to define the family?

   _____

   _____

3. Does the distinction that he makes between the family and marriage make his definition of the family clearer? Why (not)?

   _____

   _____

B. "Should Men and Women Have Different Roles?"

1. How can you tell that the author of the passage prefers the third alternative that she presents? Are there any particular words or sentences that clearly show this?

   _____

   _____

   _____

2. Do you agree with her opinion about what kind of society would be best? Why (not)?

   _____

   _____

   _____

C. "The Later Development of a Mexican Grand Family"

1. In the third paragraph, the authors describe the role of centralizing women. In this description, they use an extended metaphor of some kind of network, perhaps a computer network. Why do you think that they have chosen this metaphor? What characteristics of the centralizing women does it emphasize? Can you think of another metaphor that might also have been a good choice?

   _____

   _____

   _____

   _____

2. The main purpose of this passage is to describe changes that have taken place in the Gomez family. Why, then, do you think that the authors include the sentence that begins the fourth paragraph?

       There is a strict separation between male and female roles.

   What is its function in the essay?

   _____

   _____

D. "The Influence of Confucianism on Korean Families"

1. The section of this passage that begins on line 4 and ends on line 14 is a quotation from another work. Why do you think that the author presents it in block style rather than using quotation marks? Which method is clearer to the reader when the quoted passage is long?

   _____

   _____

2. Why do you think that the author uses this long quotation rather than putting the information into his own words?

   _____

   _____

Looking at Organization

Your teacher will tell you which of these sections to do and whether to report your answers to your partner, your group, or the whole class.

A. "The Family"

1. Which sentences in the passage actually provide a definition of the family?

_____

2. Which of these sentences is more general, and which more specific? Why do you think that they are put in this order?

_____

_____

_____

B. "Should Men and Women Have Different Roles?"

1. Why do you think that the author presents the alternative that she prefers last? Does using the final position have a strong or weak effect on the reader?

_____

_____

2. Why does she choose to present the first two alternatives in the order they are in rather than in the opposite order? Do you think that it makes a difference which order they are in?

_____

_____

C. "The Later Development of a Mexican Grand Family"

1. What is the overall organization of the passage?

comparison and contrast _____

from effect to cause _____

chronological _____

2. Why do you think that the authors chose this type of organization?

_____

_____

D. "The Influence of Confucianism on Korean Families"

1. Complete the following outline of the passage. If there is no topic sentence, write one.

   Paragraph 1 (lines 1–14):

   Topic sentence: Confucian values and norms imposed an indelible stamp on the institution of the Korean family, for they governed both intra- and interfamily relationships.

   Type of organization: General statement supported by specific examples

   Paragraph 2 (lines 15–25):

   Topic sentence: Koreans still closely attach themselves to the family.

   Type of organization: _____

   _____

   Paragraph 3 (lines 26–32):

   Topic sentence: _____

   _____

   _____

   _____

   Type of organization: _____

   _____

   Paragraph 4 (lines 33–44):

   Topic sentence: _____

   _____

   _____

   _____

   Type of organization: _____

   _____

2. Underline the sentences in the passage which show cause and effect.

3. Which of the four paragraphs contains the thesis of the passage?

   _____

4. Copy or write a thesis statement for the passage.

_____

_____

_____

5. How do the other paragraphs relate to this thesis statement?

Paragraph 1: _____

_____

_____

Paragraph 3: _____

_____

_____

Paragraph 4: _____

_____

_____

6. This passage contains four paragraphs. Suppose that you were going to expand it into ten to fifteen paragraphs. How many extra paragraphs would you add to each of the original paragraphs? What information would you put in them?

Paragraph 1:

Number of added paragraphs on this topic: _____

Added information: _____

_____

Paragraph 2:

Number of added paragraphs on this topic: _____

Added information: _____

_____

Paragraph 3:

Number of added paragraphs on this topic: _____

Added information: _____

_____

Paragraph 4:

Number of added paragraphs on this topic: _____

Added information: _____

_____

Applying What You Have Studied

■ Putting Ideas Together

Read the most recent drafts of the different sections of your partner's research paper and yours. Make a list of all of the connectors that you can find. Then, put each connector in the appropriate list.

Addition	Contrast	Cause or Effect	Support or Example

Are these connectors used correctly in your papers?

Can you add any other connectors to your lists? Do you think that any of them can be used in either of your papers to make the relationships clearer?

■ Expanding Your Ideas

Reread the drafts that you have just looked at. Draw a circle around your thesis statement. Then, read each paragraph. Underline the topic sentence if there is one, or write one in the margin. In the margin, also write the method of support that you have used in the paragraph. If you want to make any changes, do so now.

Exchange papers with your partner. Complete this section in your partner's book. (Put your name in the blank space.)

_____'s *Comments about Organization*

1. In general, I found your paper well-organized because _____

2. When I read your thesis statement, I understand what your paper is about.

    yes _____   no _____

3. Do you want to consider rewriting your thesis statement? I would word it this way: _____

    _____

    _____

4. I'm not sure that you've chosen a correct topic sentence for the following paragraphs:

    _____

    _____

    _____

5. I'm not sure that the topics of the following paragraphs relate to your thesis statement:

    _____

    _____

    _____

Read your partner's questions, comments, and suggestions. Then, discuss them with your partner, and let your partner discuss your questions, comments, and suggestions with you.

Rewrite your work on a clean piece of paper, using as many ideas from your partner as you want to. Remember that what you have written on each other's papers are *only* ideas. You don't have to follow your partner's suggestions if you don't want to, but, if you think some of the ideas will make your work better, use them. When you are finished with your work, put it away.

5. WRITING MORE

You have been writing about a topic that you chose in Chapter 4 and began to do research on. You were told to keep a record of bibliographic information about your sources. In Chapter 5, you continued your research on this topic. You also created at least one table or chart, and you wrote a tentative outline of your paper. Finally, you wrote a tentative thesis statement, introduction, and conclusions.

In this chapter, you are going to finish writing your paper. Since some of the information in your paper comes from your research, you are going to have to learn how to give credit to the sources from which you have gotten this information.

Giving Credit for Information and Ideas

Giving credit serves two major purposes. First, it acknowledges the authors or editors from whom you have gotten ideas. Second, it allows others who read your paper to find out more about your topic if it interests them.

There are several accepted ways of giving credit. The one that will be used here is that of the American Psychological Association (APA). However, if your teacher wants you to use a different method, follow his or her instructions.

An important part of a research paper is the bibliography.

> A **bibliography** is a list of books and other sources that you have used to get information and ideas for your paper.

Pages 238–239 give examples of how the APA format is used to cite books, articles in periodicals, and works that are not printed. (The examples are some of the sources used for reading passages in this textbook.) If a source that you want to use is not covered in this section, ask your teacher or librarian to help you. You can also refer to the following book:

Publication manual of the American Psychological Association (3rd ed.). (1983). Washington, DC: American Psychological Association.

■ Proper Bibliographical Form

Books or parts of books:

With one author:

Kim, I. (1981). *New urban immigrants: The Korean community in New York*. Princeton, NJ: Princeton University Press.

With two authors:

Dell'Orefice, C., & Lewis, A. A. (1985). *Staying beautiful*. New York: Harper Collins.

With no author:

Publication manual of the American Psychological Association (3rd ed.). (1983). Washington, DC: American Psychological Association.

Reprinted edition:

Mead, M. (1963). *Sex and temperament in three primitive societies*. New York: William Morrow and Company. (Original work published 1935)

Article or chapter in an edited book:

Mayer, E. (1984). A tribute to the household. In R. T. Smith (Ed.), *Kinship ideology and practice in Latin America*. (pp. 95–97). Chapel Hill, NC: University of North Carolina Press.

Articles in periodicals:

Newspaper or newspaper magazine articles:

Jones, C. (1990, August 3). Japanese leaders lament baby deficit. *The Christian Science Monitor*, p. 3.

Greenspan, B. (1991, April 21). The greater part of glory. *Parade Magazine*, pp. 3–4.

Magazine article:

Brooks, L. (1991, April). Sparkling Spanish isles. *TWA Ambassador*, pp. 28–33, 35.

Journal article with one author:

Okpala, A. O. (1989). Female employment and family size among urban Nigerian women. *Journal of Developing Areas, 23*, 439–456.

Sample Bibliography

Brooks, L. (1991, April). Sparkling Spanish isles. *TWA Ambassador*, pp. 28–33, 35.
Dell'Orefice, C., & Lewis, A. A. (1985). *Staying beautiful*. New York: Harper Collins.
Greenspan, B. (1991, April 21). The greater part of glory. *Parade Magazine*, pp. 3–4.

Jones, C. (1990, August 3). Japanese leaders lament baby deficit. *The Christian Science Monitor*, p. 3.

Kim, I. (1981). *New urban immigrants: The Korean community in New York.* Princeton, NJ: Princeton University Press.

Mayer, E. (1984). A tribute to the household. In R. T. Smith (Ed.), *Kinship ideology and practice in Latin America.* (pp. 95–97). Chapel Hill, NC: University of North Carolina Press.

Mead, M. (1963). *Sex and temperament in three primitive societies.* New York: William Morrow and Company. (Original work published 1935)

Okpala, A. O. (1989, April). Female employment and family size among urban Nigerian women. *Journal of Developing Areas, 23,* 439–456.

Publication manual of the American Psychological Association, (3rd ed.). (1983). Washington, DC: American Psychological Association.

EXERCISE: Work with your partner. Answer the questions that follow.

1. What determines the order in which bibliographic entries are listed?

   _____

2. Which line of each bibliographic entry starts at the left margin?

   _____

   Where are the other lines started?

   _____

3. Where should you put the name(s) of the author(s)?

   _____

   Which part of an author's name should you put first: the family name or the given name(s)? _____

   Which part of an author's name should you only give the initial(s) for: the family name or the given name(s)? _____

   What is the only case in which the name(s) of the author(s) do NOT begin a bibliographic entry?

   _____

   In this case, what is the first element of the bibliographic entry?

   _____

4. What information should you put after the name(s) of the author(s)?

   _____

   What punctuation marks should you put on either side of the date?

   _____

What punctuation mark comes after you close the parentheses?

_____

If the bibliographic entry is for a book, what must the date contain?

_____

What about a magazine? _____

What about a newspaper? _____
If the date in the entry contains the month, day, and year, what order should you put them in?

_____

What punctuation mark should you use? _____

Where? _____

5. What information should you put after the date?

_____

When should you underline this information to indicate italics? When shouldn't you?

_____

What parts of the title of a book, article, or chapter should you capitalize?

_____

What punctuation mark should you put after the title of a book, article, or chapter?

_____

6. If the source is a book with one or more authors, what information should you put after the title?

_____

What punctuation mark comes after the place of publication?

_____

What punctuation mark comes after the name of the publisher?

_____

7. If the source is a chapter in an edited book, what information should you put after the title of the chapter?

_____

8. If the source is an article in a periodical, what information should you put after the title of the article?

   _____

   What parts of the title of the newspaper, magazine, or journal should you capitalize?

   _____

   Should you underline or italicize this title?

   yes _____   no _____

   What punctuation mark should you put after the title of the newspaper, magazine, or journal? _____

9. If the source is an article in a newspaper or magazine, what information should you put after the title of the newspaper?

   _____

   What punctuation mark should you put after the page number(s)?

   _____

10. If the source is an article in a journal, what information should you put after the title of the journal and before the page number(s)?

    _____

    What punctuation mark should you put after the volume number?

    _____

EXERCISE: With your partner, write proper bibliographic entries for the sources that you have used or will be using in writing your research paper. When you have finished, put your entries in alphabetical order according to the family name of the first author or editor. (If there is no author or editor, alphabetize according to the title of the source.) Copy the bibliography in proper form onto a clean piece of paper and give it to your teacher.

■ Plagiarism

It probably seems that you have done enough work just writing a proper bibliography! However, believe it or not, this is only part of the job of giving credit. You must also indicate to the readers of your paper EVERY TIME that you use an idea that you have gotten from one of your sources. This is true whether you use the author's exact words, paraphrase, or simply use an idea. It does not matter.

> Whenever you use any information or words from another person's work, you must give him or her credit in the text of your paper.

Every culture or subculture has its own rules and penalties for breaking these rules. In the subculture of academic institutions in some parts of the world (and the United States is one of these places), the rules about giving credit for information or words from another person's work are very important. Failure to follow these rules has a special name: plagiarism. Moreover, the penalties for plagiarism can be quite serious. Students may be given a failing grade in a course. In some cases, they may be forced to leave the school. There have even been cases when plagiarism outside of the academic world had serious consequences. People have lost their jobs, and political candidates have been forced to step down.

■ Citations within the Text of a Paper

A citation is a way of giving credit. In the format recommended by the APA, a citation is put in parentheses. If the name of the author of the source is not mentioned in the immediate context of the citation, the citation contains the author's family name followed by a comma followed by the date of publication: (Roe, 1983). This makes it easy for the reader to find the source in the bibliography. If the name of the author is in the immediate context of the citation, then it is not given in the citation: According to Roe (1983), . . . Finally, if the information or ideas that need to be cited are found on (a) specific page(s) and not just in the whole work, the specific page(s) must be given in the citation: (Roe, 1993, p. 29). This type of citation should be used immediately after the idea or information that it refers to, immediately after the quotation marks that close a quotation, and immediately after a block quotation.

Here are some examples of the use of citations based on the passage "Should Men and Women Have Different Roles," by Margaret Mead.

> The issue of different roles for men and women can be approached from an anthropological point of view. (Mead, 1963)

> Margaret Mead (1963) has written at length on the different types of roles that can be assigned to men and women in different societies.

> Margaret Mead concludes that these roles need not be fixed, even for a particular society: ". . . the only solution of the problem [of dealing with male and female roles] does not lie between an acceptance of standardization of sex differences . . . and the abolition of these differences . . . ." (Mead, 1963, p. 319)

The only other type of citation that you may have to worry about is the type to use if you include information from a letter or conversation in your paper. These sources are called **personal communications**. If you use information from a personal communication in your paper, you should not include it in your bibliography. However, you should use the following citation form in the text of your paper: (J. A. Roe, personal communication, April 2, 1993).

EXERCISE: Work with your partner. Each of you should choose one or two pages of your paper that you have already written. (Remember, you can still change these pages or any other part later!) Work together to write citations based on your research, your bibliography, and the information or quotations that you have included. When you have finished this section, copy it onto a clean piece of paper and give it to your teacher. Your teacher's comments will help you to write better citations in your final paper.

■ Writing a Complete Draft of Your Research Paper

Decide which thesis statement you want to use for your paper. Also choose one of the introductions and conclusions that you wrote in Chapter 5 (or a different one). Use these sections, the bibliography that you have just compiled, and the outline that you wrote in Chapter 5. Write a complete draft of your paper. Be sure to use citations to give credit for the information and ideas that you have gotten from other sources. The bibliography should be the last section of your paper.

6. WRITING IT RIGHT

Study the parts of the Portfolio of Grammatical Forms, Usage, and Exercises on pages 320–324 that your teacher tells you to study. Then, proofread the draft that your partner has written. Then, complete this section in your partner's book.

1. Are connectors used correctly? Use this space to write any sentences that you think need to be changed.

_____

_____

_____

2. Are there any sentences that contain unreal conditionals? Are they used correctly? Use this space to write any sentences that you think need to be changed.

_____

_____

_____

Use this space to indicate any places where you think that unreal conditionals could be used.

_____

_____

_____

3. Do the entries in the bibliography and the citations have the proper form? Is all of the necessary information given? Use this space to write any entries and citations that you think need to be changed.

_____

_____

_____

Return your partner's last draft and take back your last draft. Study your partner's proofreading and ask any questions that you may have. Then, write another draft of your paper.

7. WRITING IT OVER

Read the draft that your partner has just written. Complete this section of your parnter's book.

1. I enjoyed reading your paper because _____

_____

_____

2. Thank you. I have learned a lot about _____

_____

_____

_____

3. I would like to suggest that you make the following change:

_____

_____

_____

4. Please check the following information:

_____

_____

_____

_____

Is it possible that you forgot to give credit?

Give back your partner's paper and take back your own paper. Read your partner's suggestions and questions, and think about them. You may also decide that you want to add or eliminate some information. Then, write another draft of your essay. Give this final draft to your teacher.

8. MORE WRITING

In this chapter, this section consists of a list of topics that you may want to use for doing another research paper. Follow your teacher's instructions about using it.

1. Changes that have taken place in _____

2. What has been happening to the air we breathe

3. The causes of _____

4. The influence of _____ on the history of

_____

9. PERSONAL GLOSSARY

Use the space provided to write any words that you have learned in this chapter. Also write a definition for each word.

Portfolios

Portfolio of Word Forms and Exercises

WORD FORMS FOUND IN THIS SECTION

FROM CHAPTER 1

    A. Adjectives with the suffix *-ful*
    B. Nouns with the suffix *-ship*

FROM CHAPTER 2

    A. Nouns with the suffix *-tion*
    B. Verbs with the suffix *-ate*
    C. Other nouns with the suffix *-tion*

FROM CHAPTER 3

    A. Nouns that end in *-nce* and adjectives that end in *-nt*
    B. Adjectives with the suffix *-ive*

FROM CHAPTER 4

    A. People and what they study and believe in
    B. Nouns and verbs that have the same spelling

FROM CHAPTER 5

    A. Nouns with the suffix *-ity*
    B. Verbs with the suffix *-ify*
    C. Adjectives with the suffix *-ous*

FROM CHAPTER 6

    A. Verbs with the suffix *-ize*
    B. Making nouns from verbs that have the suffix *-ize*
    C. Adjectives that end in *-ry*

FROM CHAPTER 1

A. Adjectives with the Suffix *-ful*

1. Which word in line 23 of "The Making of a Scientist" ends in the suffix *-ful*?

   _____

   Which word in line 44? _____

2. What part of speech are these two words?

   nouns _____   adjectives _____

   verbs _____   adverbs _____

3. What part of speech are *success* and *wonder*?

   nouns _____   adjectives _____

   verbs _____   adverbs

4. Write a rule that describes how to use the suffix *-ful* to change a noun into an adjective.

   _____

   _____

   _____

5. Complete the following table. Use other words that you and your partner know to fill in the last two pairs of blanks.

Noun	Adjective that ends in *-ful*
_____	beautiful
care	_____
_____	fearful
success	_____
_____	wonderful
_____	_____
_____	_____

B. Nouns with the Suffix *-ship*

1. Which word in line 26 of the passage ends in the suffix *-ship*?

   _____

2. What part of speech is this word?

   noun _____   adjective _____

   verb _____   adverb _____

3. What part of speech is *relation*?

   noun _____   adjective _____

   verb _____   adverb _____

4. Complete the following table. Use words that you and your partner know to fill in the last two pairs of blanks.

Noun	Noun that ends in *-ship*
friend	_____
_____	leadership
relation	_____
_____	_____
_____	_____

FROM CHAPTER 2

A. Nouns with the Suffix *-tion*

1. Which word in line 4 of "The Tradition Lives On" ends in the suffix *-tion*?

_____

2. Which word in line 6 ends in the same suffix?

_____

3. What part of speech are these two words: nouns, verbs, or adjectives?

_____

How can you tell? What are their functions in the sentences that they occur in?

_____

_____

B. Verbs with the Suffix *-ate*

1. What verb does the noun *operation* come from?

   _____

2. What verb does the noun *location* come from?

   _____

3. Work with your partner to write a rule that describes how to make a noun out of a verb that ends in the letters *-ate*.

   _____

   _____

4. What noun can you make from the verb *concentrate*?

   _____

C. Other Nouns with the Suffix *-tion*

1. What verb does the noun *continuation* come from?

   _____

2. How does the formation of *continuation* from *continue* differ from the formation of *operation, location,* and *concentration*?

   _____

   _____

3. What part of speech is the word *tradition*, used in the title of the passage?

   _____

   Can you find any corresponding verb in your dictionary?

   _____

   What does this tell you about some nouns that end in *-tion*?

   _____

4. When a word ends in the letters *-ate*, what part of speech is it?

   _____

5. When a word ends in the suffix *-tion*, what part of speech is it?

   _____

FROM CHAPTER 3

A. Nouns That End in *-nce* and Adjectives That End in *-nt*

1. In lines 21–22 of "The German Who Helped Jesse Owens," the word *magnificently* is used to describe the way Jesse Owens leaped. What part of speech is *magnificently*?

   noun _____

   verb _____

   adverb _____

   What adjective does it come from? _____

2. "The magnificence of Owens' leap must have amazed the audience at the Berlin Olympics." In this sentence, what part of speech is the word *magnificence*?

   noun _____

   verb _____

   adverb _____

3. What part of speech is *distance* in line 9 of "The German Who Helped Jesse Owens"? _____

   What adjective is it related to? _____

4. With your partner, use the space below to write a rule for changing an adjective that ends in *-nt* to a noun.

   _____

   _____

   _____

5. In line 4 of "The Incident of the Hair," Carmen says that she complied with Richard's wishes. We can also say that she tried to be compliant.

   What noun is related to the adjective *compliant*?

   _____

6. What noun can be made from the word *insignificant* in lines 5–6?

   _____

B. Adjectives with the Suffix *-ive*

1. What part of speech is *progressive* in line 9 of "The Incident of the Hair"?

    noun _____

    adjective _____

    adverb _____

    What verb does it come from? _____

2. What part of speech is *expression* in line 25 of "The Incident of the Hair"?

    _____

    What verb does it come from? _____

    What adjective can be made from this verb?

    _____

3. With your partner, write two rules. Write one for changing a verb that ends in *-ess* to an adjective. Write another for changing a verb that ends in *-ess* to a noun.

    _____

    _____

    _____

    _____

    _____

4. What part of speech is the word *hypersensitive* in line 19 of "The Incident of the Hair"? _____
    (The prefix *hyper-* means *overly* or *too*.)

    What about the word *sensitive*? _____

5. What verb is the adjective *sensitive* related to? (Look in your dictionary or ask your teacher if you don't know.) _____

    What does this show about the relationship between some adjectives that end in *-ive* and the verbs that they come from?

    _____

    _____

FROM CHAPTER 4

A. People and What They Study and Believe In

1. What part of speech is the word *political* in line 1 of "Japanese Leaders

   Lament Baby Deficit"? _____

   How do you know?

   _____

   _____

   There are two nouns that are related to the adjective *political: politics* and
   politician.

   Which one describes a person? _____

   Which one describes the field that that person practices in?

   _____

   Complete each of the following sentences:

   A politician _____.

   Politics _____.

   Is the word *politician* singular or plural? _____

   What about *politics*? _____

   Can you think of any other words that end in the letter *-s* but are singular?
   What are they?

   _____

   _____

2. In line 7 of "Female Employment and Family Size," what part of speech is

   the word *economic*? _____

   Write a form of this word that describes a field of study.

   _____

   What is a person who studies or practices in this field called?

   _____

   What other adjective is related to *economics, economist,* and *economic*?

   _____

What is the difference in meaning between *economic* and *economical*?

_____

_____

3. Complete the following table.

Area of Study	Person	Adjective
demographics	demographer	demographic
_____	_____	economic/ economical
_____	ethicist	_____
physics	_____	_____
_____	_____	political
_____	statistician	_____

4. What part of speech is *logical* in line 1 of "The Broadnaxes: A Modern American Family"? _____

   What noun describes the area of study that this adjective applies to?

   _____

   How is this noun different from *demographics, physics,* and the other area of study nouns in Question 3?

   _____

   _____

   What noun describes a person involved in this area?

   _____

5. What part of speech is the word *survival* in line 3 of "Japanese Leaders Lament Baby Deficit"? _____

   How do you know?

   _____

   _____

6. Are all English words that end in -*al* the same part of speech? _____

7. What word does *survival* come from? _____

   What part of speech is *survive*? _____

   What noun can you make from the verb *deny* (*denied* in line 11 of

   "Japanese Leaders Lament Baby Deficit")? _____

8. What part of speech is *clerical* in line 2 of "Female Employment and

   Family Size"? _____

   What noun is it related to? _____

9. What part of speech is *managerial* in line 3 of "Female Employment and

   Family Size"? _____

   What noun is it related to? _____

   What verb? _____

10. What part of speech is the word *ministries* in line 4 of "Female Employ-

    ment and Family Size"? _____

    Is it singular or plural? _____

    How do you know?

    _____

    _____

    What is the singular form? _____

    What adjective is related to it? _____

11. Are all adjectives that end in -*al* related to nouns that end in -*ics* or -*ic*?

    _____

12. What part of speech is *sexist* in line 1 of "Japanese Leaders Lament Baby

    Deficit"? _____

    How do you know?

    _____

    _____

    What noun describes a person who is sexist?

    _____

What noun describes the beliefs of sexists?

_____

13. What part of speech is *feminists* in line 9 of "Japanese Leaders Lament Baby Deficit"? _____

How do you know?

_____

_____

What adjective describes someone who is a feminist?

_____

What noun describes the beliefs of feminists?

_____

14. Complete the following table:

Belief	Person	Adjective
capitalism	_____	_____
_____	communist	_____
_____	_____	feminist
_____	sexist	_____

B. Nouns and Verbs That Have the Same Spelling

1. What part of speech is the word *comment* in line 12 of "Japanese Leaders Lament Baby Deficit"? _____

How do you know?

_____

_____

What is the verb that is related to this word?

_____

2. What noun in line 13 of "Japanese Leaders Lament Baby Deficit" has the same form as a verb? _____

3. What noun in line 22 of "Female Employment and Family Size" has the same form as a verb? _____

4. Make a list of other English nouns and verbs that share the same written form.

Noun	Verb
_____	_____
_____	_____
_____	_____
_____	_____

FROM CHAPTER 5

A. Nouns with the Suffix *-ity*

1. Write the words that end in *-ity* in each of the following passages and lines.

"Female Employment in Western Europe"

(17) _____

"Holding up the Sky"

(16) _____

"Women and the Labor Market: The Link Grows Stronger"

(15) _____

(18) _____

What part of speech are these words? _____

How can you tell?

_____

_____

2. To what part of speech is the suffix *-ity* usually added to make a noun?

_____

Is it always added to an adjective? _____

Give one or two examples in which it is not.

_____

_____

Do you think that *opportune* is an adjective? _____

Why (not)? _____

_____

B. Verbs with the Suffix *-ify*

1. What word ends in *-ify* in line (18) of "Holding up the Sky"?

_____

What part of speech is this word? _____

How can you tell?

_____

Look the word up in a dictionary. What is its corresponding noun form?

_____

Write a rule for changing a verb that ends in the suffix *-ify* to a noun.

_____

_____

_____

2. Complete the following table:

Verb ending in -*ify*	Noun
classify	_____
_____	clarification
electrify	_____
_____	pacification
verify	_____
_____	_____
_____	_____

C. Adjectives with the Suffix -*ous*

1. Write the words that contain -*ous*- in each of the following passages and lines.

   "Paying Tribute to the Encomendero: An Indian's Point of View"

   (7) _____

   "Female Employment in Western Europe"

   (12) _____

   "Women and the Labor Market: The Link Grows Stronger"

   (75) _____

2. What part of speech are the second two words? _____

   How can you tell?

   _____

   How can you make the first word into an adjective?

   _____

FROM CHAPTER 6

A. Verbs with the Suffix *-ize*

1. Which word in line 1 of "The Family" contains the suffix *-ize*?

   _____

   What part of speech is this word? _____

   How can you tell?

   _____

   What noun has the suffix *-ize* been added to? _____

2. What other verbs that end in *-ize* are on the following lines of "Should Men and Women Have Different Roles"?

   4: _____

   13: _____

   30: _____

3. Can you find a verb form that comes from a verb ending in *-ize* on line 30 of "Should Men and Women Have Different Roles?"? _____ What is it?

   _____

   Why doesn't this form contain the letter *e* after *iz*?

   _____

4. In "The Later Development of a Mexican Grand Family," what verb with the suffix *-ize* occurs on line 16? _____

   On line 36? _____

B. Making Nouns from Verbs That Have the Suffix *-ize*

1. You found the verb *standardize* on line 4 of "Should Men and Women Have Different Roles" What related word is on line 26?

   _____

What part of speech is this word? _____

How can you tell? _____

_____

Write a rule for changing a verb that has the suffix *-ize* into a noun that ends in *-tion*:

_____

_____

_____

2. What noun that ends in *-ization* is on line 28 of "Should Men and Women

   Have Different Roles?" _____

   What nouns that end in *-ization* are on line 27 of "The Influence of Confucianism on Korean Families"?

   _____, _____, and

   _____

3. Complete the following tables.

Adjective	Verb	Noun that Describes a Process
_____	centralize	_____
_____	civilize	_____
industrial	_____	_____
_____	modernize	_____
_____	penalize	_____
special	_____	_____
_____	_____	urbanization

Noun	Verb	Noun that Describes a Process
character	_____	_____
XXXXXXXXXX	_____	recognition

4. Do all verbs that end in the suffix -*ize* come from adjectives?

   yes _____   no _____

5. Do all verbs that end in the suffix -*ize* form nouns that end in -*ation*?

   yes _____   no _____

C. Adjectives That End in -*ry*

1. What words that end in the suffix -*ary* are on the following lines of "Should Men and Women Have Different Roles"?

   5: _____

   29: _____

   40: _____

   What part of speech are these words? _____

   How can you tell?

   _____

   What words that end in the suffix -*ary* are on the following lines of "The Influence of Confucianism on Korean Families"?

   5: _____

   20: _____

2. What word that ends in -*ry* is on line 10 of "The Later Development of a Mexican Grand Family"? _____

   What vowel comes before the -*ry*? _____

3. Use the space provided to list some other adjectives that end in *-ary, -ery*, or *-ory*.

_____

_____

_____

_____

_____

Portfolio of Grammatical Forms, Usage, and Exercises

GRAMMATICAL FORMS AND USAGE ILLUSTRATED AND PRACTICED IN THIS SECTION

FROM CHAPTER 1

    A. *Used to* and *would*
    B. *Enough* and *too*
    C. Using colons
    D. Tense consistency
    E. Correct written sentence word order

FROM CHAPTER 2

    A. The present perfect progressive
    B. The simple present perfect
    C. *Since* and *for*
    D. Adverbial in sentence-initial position

FROM CHAPTER 3

    A. The simple past perfect
    B. The past perfect progressive
    C. Modal perfects
    D. *So . . . that*

FROM CHAPTER 4

    A. Infinitives and gerunds
       1. Perfect infinitives and gerunds
       2. Gerunds as nouns
       3. Infinitives in sentences with "empty" *it* as subject
    B. *Each* and *every*

C. Real conditionals
   1. Present real conditionals
   2. Future real conditionals
   3. Past real conditionals

FROM CHAPTER 5

A. Distinguishing between contrast and support
B. Different ways of showing contrast
C. The passive voice
D. Reduced adjective clauses that contain present and past participle adjectives

FROM CHAPTER 6
Unreal or hypothetical conditionals
   1. Present unreal conditionals
   2. Future unreal conditionals
   3. Past unreal conditionals

FROM CHAPTER 1

A. *Used to* and *Would*

Look at the following chart:

Action	Continued State or Feeling
When I was a child, my brother and I used to go to the movies once a week.	We used to enjoy seeing children's movies.
When I was a child, my brother and I would go to the movies once a week.	XXXXXXXXXX

What kinds of past actions and states or feelings do all of the sentences describe?

those that occurred just once _____

those that occurred more than once _____

Both *used to* and *would* describe actions that occurred regularly or over a certain period of time in the past. They can both be used in this function. However, usually only *used to* can be used with verbs that describe a continued state or feeling.

EXERCISE: Read each sentence that contains *used to*. If the verb describes an action, rewrite the sentence using *would*. If it describes a continued state or feeling, write "No change is possible." The first two are done for you.

1. When I was a child, we used to visit my grandmother (my father's mother) almost every weekend. When I was a child, we would visit my grandmother every weekend.

2. I used to like the smells that came from her kitchen when we arrived. No change is possible.

3. She used to bake several cakes before we came. _____

_____

4. The cakes used to be cooling on the kitchen table when we got there. ____

_____

5. I used to be her only granddaughter. _____

_____

(This was until my aunt gave birth to twin girls when I was ten years old.)

6. She always used to tell me that she was happy that I was a girl. _____

_____

7. I used to have long brown hair. _____

_____

8. She used to tell me how pretty my hair was. _____

_____

9. I used to sit on her lap while she brushed my hair. _____

_____

10. I always used to be happy when I was with her. _____

_____

Study these negative sentences:

1. Our parents would not go to the movies with us.

2. a. They did not use to enjoy children's movies.
   b. They used not to enjoy children's movies.

   Write a description of how to make negative statements with *would*:

   _____

   _____

   Write two descriptions of how to make negative statements with *used to*.

   _____

   _____

EXERCISE: Read each sentence. If the state or action that one or more of the verbs describes occurred regularly or over a certain period of time in the past, change the verb(s) to *used to* or *would* plus the simple form. Otherwise, write "No change is possible." The first three are done for you.

1. Sometimes, we stayed home on weekends. Sometimes, we used to stay home on weekends. OR Sometimes, we would stay home on weekends.

2. My grandmother was often in poor health. My grandmother often used to be in poor health.

3. One Saturday, she wasn't waiting when we got to her home. No change is possible.

4. She was in the hospital. _____

   _____

5. We almost never called her before we came. _____

   _____

6. We only called to say we weren't coming. _____

   _____

7. We always expected her to be there. _____

   _____

8. This particular Saturday, I was very surprised when she wasn't there, and no cakes were cooling on the kitchen table. _____

   _____

9. My father called my aunt, who told him my grandmother was in the hospital. _____

_____

10. For years afterward, I always remembered how frightened I was on that day. _____

_____

B. *Enough* and *Too*

Study the chart. Then answer the questions that follow.

Sentences That Contain *Too*	Sentences That Contain *Enough*
Did the dinosaur run too slowly to catch the small animals?	Did the small animals run quickly enough to escape from the dinosaur?
The dinosaur's head was too big to fit into the window.	The dinosaur was tall enough to reach the window.
Feynman had too many interests to be bored.	Feynman asked enough questions to keep his parents busy.

1. Which parts of speech can *too* occur before?

    nouns _____   adjectives _____

    verbs _____   adverbs _____

2. Which parts of speech can *enough* occur after?

    nouns _____   adjectives _____

    verbs _____   adverbs _____

3. Which part of speech can *enough* occur before?

    nouns _____   adjectives _____

    verbs _____   adverbs _____

4. What form of the verb occurs after phrases that contain *too* or *enough*?

_____

EXERCISE: Combine each pair of sentences to make one sentence that contains *too* or *enough*. The first two are done for you.

1. Feynman's father had some information about physics.
   He was able to ask a question about photons.
   <u>Feynman's father had enough information about physics to ask a question about photons.</u>

2. Perhaps Feynman was very inexperienced.
   He could not answer the question.
   <u>Perhaps Feynman was too inexperienced to answer the question.</u>

3. Perhaps he explained very quickly.
   He couldn't make his father understand.

   _____

   _____

4. The other fathers felt they had very little time.
   They did not want to take their children for walks.

   _____

   _____

5. Feynman's father had time.
   He took his son for walks.

   _____

   _____

6. Feynman studied hard.
   He got into MIT.

   _____

   _____

7. Feynman and his wife's family had money.
   They were able to take good care of her.

   _____

   _____

C. Using Colons

Compare these four sentences. Then, with your partner, answer the questions that follow.

    a. Feynman felt bad because he could not answer his father's question.

    b. Because he could not answer his father's question, Feynman felt bad.

    c. Feynman felt bad; he could not answer his father's question.

    d. Feynman felt bad for one reason: he could not answer his father's question.

1. Which sentence ends in a clause that cannot be an independent sentence?

    _____

2. Which sentence begins with a clause that cannot be an independent sentence? _____

3. Which sentences contain two clauses, each of which could be an independent sentence? _____ and _____

    In which of these is the second clause equivalent to a word that comes before it? _____

4. Write a rule for using (and not using) a comma in a sentence which contains one independent clause and one dependent clause.

    _____

    _____

    _____

    _____

5. Write a rule for using a semicolon in a sentence that contains two independent clauses.

    _____

    _____

    _____

    _____

6. Write a rule for using a colon in a sentence that contains two independent clauses.

    _____

    _____

    _____

    _____

EXERCISE: Each group of words below can be punctuated as *one sentence* that contains a comma, a semicolon, a colon, or no internal punctuation. Write each sentence, beginning with a capital letter and correctly punctuated, in the space provided. The first four are done for you.

1. until the end of his life, Feynman continued to learn more and more about his main area of study physics interested him until his death
   Until the end of his life, Feynman continued to learn more and more about his main area of study: physics interested him until his death.

2. because he was a respected physicist the United States government asked him to sit on an important panel
   Because he was a respected physicist, the United States government asked him to sit on an important panel.

3. he accepted the invitation although his health was not good
   He accepted the invitation although his health was not good.

4. the panel investigated the explosion of the space shuttle Challenger in January 1986 its job was very important
   The panel investigated the explosion of the space shuttle Challenger in January 1986; its job was very important.

5. being on the panel was an important job the entire nation was interested in its findings

   _____

   _____

   _____

6. it is possible that Feynman made some people uncomfortable since he did not agree with their conclusions

   _____

   _____

   _____

7. many people first heard of Feynman because of his being on the panel it was a position that caused people to notice him

   _____

   _____

   _____

8. before he accepted the position he tried to find someone to tell him not to take it

_____

_____

_____

9. he didn't like the idea of working for the government he tried to think of excuses not to serve on the panel

_____

_____

_____

10. he probably accepted the position for one reason he thought he could make an important contribution

_____

_____

_____

D. Tense Consistency

Each pair or group of sentences can be used in casual spoken English. However, the use of a present form to describe something in the past is incorrect in formal written English. Rewrite each pair or group so that it is correct formal written English. The first one is done for you.

1. The other day, my friend and I were talking about the structure of the atom. She says, "The subject isn't very complicated." I reply, "I'm having trouble understanding photons."
   The other day, my friend and I were talking about the structure of the atom. She said, "The subject isn't very complicated." I replied, "I'm having trouble understanding photons."

2. I didn't expect to see a model of a dinosaur at the museum. It really surprised me. I'm walking around the corner, and there it is, as big as life.

   _____

   _____

   _____

3. My brother said that he was going to buy an encyclopedia for his family. I say, "Why don't you get them a computer instead?"

_____

_____

_____

4. I was walking around the library, looking for a simple book about the structure of the atom. All of a sudden, I run into Jane, whom I haven't seen in two months.

_____

_____

_____

5. I told her that I wanted to talk with her, but that I was really busy. She says, "Me, too. I'm having a tough time with physics."

_____

_____

_____

E. Correct Written Sentence Word Order

EXERCISE: Unscramble each group of words to make a correct sentence. The first one is done for you.

1. to Feynman everything learn wanted he could
   Feynman wanted to learn everything he could.

2. in enjoyed draw he forties to when he learning was his

   _____

3. study he appreciated the cultures of other

   _____

4. time music lot he a playing spent of

   _____

5. other liked he himself especially languages teaching

   _____

FROM CHAPTER 2

A. The Present Perfect Progressive

Underline the verb in the following sentence from the reading:

> For over fifty years, Bonatt's Bakery has been serving the bakery needs of Cape Codders and summer visitors alike.

The complete verb in this sentence is *has been serving*. It is the present perfect progressive form of the verb *serve*. It describes an action that began in the past and is still going on. The prepositional phrase, *for over fifty years,* tells the reader the length of time that Bonatt's Bakery has been serving people's bakery needs.

EXERCISE: Read the following information about Mark Plimpton. Then answer each question with a complete sentence. The first one is done for you.

> Mark Plimpton is a college student at Northeastern University, but he is from Harwichport, Massachusetts. His family has been living there for about 150 years. In fact, his parents live in the same house that his mother's ancestors built in 1845.
>
> Mark's father is a plumber. He has his own company. He has been working for himself since he finished school. Mark's mother is a clerk in a grocery store. She started working there when the store opened in 1988.

1. How long has Mark Plimpton's family been living in Harwichport?
   <u>They have been living there for about 150 years.</u>

2. Do they live in a house or an apartment?

   _____

   _____

3. How long have they been living there?

   _____

   _____

4. Which members of his family work?

   _____

   _____

5. Who does his father work for?

_____

_____

6. How long has he been working for himself?

_____

_____

7. Where does his mother work?

_____

_____

8. How long has she been working there?

_____

_____

EXERCISE: Answer these questions about your home town or city or the place where your family lives now. Answer each question with at least one complete sentence.

1. How long has your family been living in _____?

_____

_____

2. Do they live in a house or an apartment?

_____

_____

3. How long have they been living there?

_____

_____

4. Which members of your family work?

_____

_____

5. Where do they work?

_____

_____

6. How long have they been working there?

_____

_____

7. What is an important industry in _____?

_____

_____

8. What does this industry produce or do?

_____

_____

9. How long has the _____
   industry been _____?

_____

_____

B. The Simple Present Perfect

On page 46, Questions 5 and 6 were about the verb in the second line of the following sentence from the reading:

> Now, fifty-one years later, established in our bright new home at the Port Centre on Main Street in Harwichport, Bonatt's Bakery has grown into a tradition in its own right and is indeed part of Cape Cod lore.

As you discussed, the verb *has grown* is made up of two words. It is the simple present perfect form of the verb *grow*.

Unlike the present perfect progressive, this simple present perfect verb focuses on a result, not a process.

The simple present perfect consists of two parts: the present form of the verb *have* that agrees with the subject and a past participle.

Subject	Present Form of *Have (Not)*	Past Participle	Rest of Sentence
I	have	visited	Cape Cod.
You	have not	gone	there.
Mark	has	lived	on Cape Cod all his life.
We	have not	seen	pictures of Cape Cod before.
Linda and Marcia	have	known	each other for about ten years.

EXERCISE: Use the information given to complete a sentence that contains the simple present perfect form of the verb in parentheses. The first one is done for you.

1. The shops in Harwichport look different from the way they looked twenty years ago. (change)
   Harwichport's shops <u>have changed in the last twenty years.</u>

2. Bonnatt's Bakery was on Bank Street. Now, it is at the Port Centre on Main Street. (move)

   Bonatt's Bakery _____

   _____

3. Nowadays, more tourists come to Harwichport than before. (increase)

   The number of tourists _____

   _____

4. There are several new shops in the town. (open)

   Several new shops _____

   _____

5. Some of the older shops are not in business any more. (close)

   Some of the older shops _____

   _____

> Some English verbs do not normally occur in the progressive. Verbs that describe a state, perception, or feeling usually occur in the simple form rather than in the progressive.
>
> Use the simple present perfect in describing the length of time a state, perception, or feeling has lasted.

EXERCISE: Fill in each blank with the simple present perfect form of the verb in parentheses. The first one is done for you.

1. Mark Plimpton is studying biology at Northeastern University because he (want) <u>has wanted</u> to be a marine biologist ever since he can remember.

2. Because he was raised on Cape Cod, he (know) _____ a lot about the ocean for most of his life.

3. However, he (have) _____ a lot of questions about marine life since he was in elementary school.

4. For a long time, his parents and teachers (expect) _____ him to study biology.

5. According to his father, his family always (love) _____ the ocean.

6. They (see) _____ him read books about sea animals since he was little.

7. They (hear) _____ him ask questions that they could not answer for a long time.

8. For a long time, it (seem) _____ natural to them that he would go to college to try to find the answers.

C. *Since* and *For*

With your partner, compare these sentences and answer the questions that follow.

a. Cape Codders have been buying baked goods at Bonatt's since 1939.

b. Cape Codders have been buying baked goods at Bonatt's for over fifty years.

Answer these questions about the sentences with your partner:

1. Do sentences (a) and (b) mean the same thing?

   yes _____   no _____

2. Which phrase describes the starting point of the action?

   since 1939 _____

   for over fifty years _____

3. Which phrase describes the duration (length of time) of the action?

   since 1939 _____

   for over fifty years _____

EXERCISE: Fill in each blank with either *since* or *for*. The first two are done for you.

1. Mark Plimpton has been a student at Northeastern University <u>for</u> two years.

2. His family has been living in Harwichport <u>since</u> before the Civil War.

3. Mark writes to Linda Fletcher and Marcia Goldberg regularly. He has known them _____ they worked in Harwichport two summers ago.

4. Linda and Marcia have been friends _____ almost ten years.

5. They have been students at Northeastern University _____ about two years.

6. Linda is studying engineering because she has wanted to be an engineer _____ she was a child.

7. Marcia is majoring in drama because she has wanted to be an actress _____ a long time.

D. Adverbial in Sentence-initial Position

With your partner, compare these pairs of sentences and answer the questions that follow.

1a. Bonatt's Bakery has been serving the bakery needs of Cape Codders and summer visitors alike for over fifty years.

1b. For over fifty years, Bonatt's Bakery has been serving the bakery needs of Cape Codders and summer visitors alike.

2a. They would serve breakfast, lunch, and dinner, six days a week during those summer days.
2b. During those summer days, they would serve breakfast, lunch, and dinner, six days a week.

3a. *Boston Magazine* named Bonatt's as the "Best Bakery on Cape Cod" just this year.
3b. Just this year, *Boston Magazine* named Bonatt's as the "Best Bakery on Cape Cod."

Answer the following questions with your partner:

1. Where does the adverbial phrase occur in each (a) sentence?

    at the beginning of the sentence _____

    at the end of the sentence _____

2. Where does the adverbial phrase occur in each (b) sentence?

    at the beginning of the sentence _____

    at the end of the sentence _____

3. When an adverbial phrase occurs at the beginning of a sentence, what punctuation mark comes after it?

    a period _____

    a comma _____

    nothing _____

4. What is being emphasized when an adverbial phrase occurs at the beginning of a sentence?

    the adverbial phrase _____

    the rest of the sentence _____

EXERCISE: Rewrite each of the sentences in the exercise on page 282 to begin with the adverbial phrase. Be sure to punctuate correctly. The first two are done for you.

1. For two years, Mark Plimpton has been a student at Northeastern University.

2. Since before the Civil War, his family has been living in Harwichport.

3. _____

_____

4. _____

_____

5. _____

_____

6. _____

_____

7. _____

_____

FROM CHAPTER 3

A. The Simple Past Perfect

> The **simple present perfect** consists of a present form of the verb *have* plus a past participle.

The **simple past perfect** consists of

_____ plus _____

> In sentences that contain the **simple present perfect**, the present form of the verb *have* agrees with its subject. The form of the verb *have* (changes/does not change) _____ in the **simple past perfect** because
>
> _____
>
> _____ .

EXERCISE: Combine each pair of sentences to make one sentence that contains a past perfect verb form. Use the word or words in parentheses in your new sentence. Be sure to use the past perfect to describe the event that took place earlier. The first one is done for you.

1. Carmen decided to see how her hair looked in its natural color. Richard noticed that she had some gray hair. (when) <u>Carmen had decided to see how her hair looked in its natural color when Richard noticed that she had some gray hair.</u>

2. Carmen expected Richard to embrace her. He pulled a gray hair out of her head. (before)

   _____

   _____

   _____

3. Jesse Owens fouled on one of his tries. Lutz Long suggested that he mark the foul line with a towel. (so)

   _____

   _____

   _____

4. Owens and Lutz competed at the Olympics. They practiced a lot before the games. (when, already)

   _____

   _____

   _____

5. Lutz gained respect as a good sportsman. He was killed during World War II. (before)

   _____

   _____

   _____

EXERCISE: Here is a list of events and when they took place. With your partner, write sentences that mention at least two of these events and that contain a past perfect verb form. Do not use dates in your sentences. You may choose any events that you want to write sentences about. One is done for you.

ca. 3500 B.C.*	People who were living in the Tigris-Euphrates River Valley developed the first phonetic writing system.
ca. 2000 B.C.	The study of astronomy began in Babylon, China, Egypt, and India.
ca. 1000 B.C.	The Olmec civilization in Mexico developed a writing system.
ca. 800 B.C.	The Greek poet Homer told his famous stories.
753 B.C.	Rome was founded.
ca. 215 B.C.	The Chinese built their Great Wall.

1. The Olmec civilization in Mexico had developed a writing system before the Greek poet Homer told his famous stories.

2. _____

_____

_____

3. _____

_____

_____

4. _____

_____

_____

5. _____

_____

_____

*The abbreviation *ca.* stands for the Latin word *circa*, which means "at approximately that time." In much of the western world, the letters B.C., which stand for "before Christ," are used for dates before the birth of Christ. These dates are counted "backwards," so 1000 B.C. is earlier than 500 B.C., for example. In some countries, the letters B.C.E. ("before the Christian era") are used for this same time period. Dates after the birth of Christ are often written without any letters after them, but the letters A.D. (Latin *anno Domini*—"in the year of our Lord") can be used. In countries that use the letters B.C.E., the letters C.E. ("Christian era") are used for this period.

B. The Past Perfect Progressive

Compare the following sentences:

a. Carmen was dyeing her hair when she married Richard.

b. Carmen had been dyeing her hair for more than ten years when she married Richard.

In sentence (a), the past progressive verb form shows that the action (dyeing her hair) was taking place when Carmen married Richard. In sentence (b), the past perfect progressive verb form shows that the action had been taking place for a certain period of time (ten years) when Carmen married Richard.

A **past perfect progressive** verb form consists of these three parts:

_____ plus _____ plus

_____

EXERCISE: Add the time expression in parentheses to each sentence and rewrite the past progressive verb form as a past perfect progressive. The first one is done for you.

1. Mark was sleeping when Tom called. (half an hour) <u>Mark had been sleeping for half an hour when Tom called.</u>

2. Tom was waiting for Linda when he met Marcia. (ten minutes)

_____

3. Linda and Marcia were studying in the library when they saw their teacher. (several hours)

_____

_____

4. Marcia was watching television when Linda got home. (over an hour)

_____

_____

5. Tom was waiting for the mail when he got a postcard from his father. (only a few minutes)

_____

_____

_____

EXERCISE: Complete each sentence about yourself and the person or people you are living with. Use a past progressive verb form in each sentence.

1. I _____ for _____

_____ when _____home.

2. My _____ for _____

when _____.

3. When _____,

_____.

C. Modal Perfects

Read the following sentences:

Without Lutz's towel, Jesse Owens <u>might not have won</u> the championship. On the other hand, he <u>might have won</u> anyhow. Who knows?

> The verb forms _might have won_ and _might not have won_ are called **modal perfects.**

1. Why do you think that they are called _modals_?

_____

_____

2. Why do you think that they are called _perfects_? What do they have in common with the past perfect and the present perfect?

_____

_____

3. Do modals change their form according to their subject?

   yes _____

   no _____

4. What kind of verb form comes after a modal?

   the infinitive _____

   the present participle _____

   the simple form _____

5. If a modal is negative, where is *not* or *n't* put?

   _____

   _____

6. What kind of verb form comes after a form of the verb *have* in a perfect verb form?

   the past participle _____

   the present participle _____

   the infinitive _____

7. Work with your partner to write a rule for making modal perfect verb forms:

   A modal perfect verb form consists of these three parts:

   _____ plus _____ plus

   _____

   A negative modal perfect verb form consists of these four parts:

   _____ plus _____ plus

   _____ plus _____

   A modal perfect verb form (changes/does not change) _____ according to

   its subject because _____

   _____

   _____

EXERCISE: Read the following story. Then answer each of the questions with at least one complete sentence.

During Tom's last year of high school, he received a two-seater sports car for his birthday. The car was very small. It had only two seats: one for the driver and one for the passenger. However, it was exactly what Tom had wanted for a long time, and he really enjoyed it. He and his girlfriend, Sarah, used to go for rides in it whenever they had the time.

One day, after Tom had had the car for a couple of months, he was driving alone down a street near his home. All of a sudden, although the weather report had predicted a clear day, it started to rain very heavily. Tom continued driving until he had to stop at a red light near a bus stop. It was really raining quite hard.

The light was long, and Tom turned his head in the direction of the bus stop. He saw three people standing there: Sarah, a middle-aged friend of his mother's, and an old man who looked sick. Sarah was waving and calling his name. None of them had an umbrella, and all of them were quite wet. There wasn't a bus in sight.

1. What could Tom have done in this situation?

_____

_____

_____

2. Could he have done anything else?

_____

_____

_____

3. What couldn't he have done?

_____

_____

_____

4. What should he have done?

_____

_____

_____

Why? _____

_____

5. What would you have done in Tom's situation?

_____

_____

_____

Why? _____

_____

6. Would your partner have done the same thing?

_____

Why or why not? _____

_____

_____

_____

Now answer these questions.

1. Which modal perfect is used to show past possibility?

   could have _____

   should have _____

   would have _____

2. Which one is used to show past impossibility?

   could not have _____

   should not have _____

   would not have _____

3. Which one is used to show the desirability of an action in the past?

   could have _____

   should have _____

   would have _____

EXERCISE: Now read this science fiction story. Then answer each of the questions that follow with at least one complete sentence.

Captain Temple had landed her small space ship on the planet Medusa. She was alone, and it was her mission to contact a representative of the ruling class on the planet. Unfortunately, although there were only two groups of people on the planet—rulers and servants—all of them looked alike, at least to Captain Temple and the alliance that she represented.

Fortunately, there was one important difference between the rulers and servants on Medusa. The servants always told the truth and the rulers always lied. Therefore, Captain Temple expected her job to be easy. She would find a Medusan and ask him a question. If he answered correctly, she would know that he was a servant. If he lied, she would know that he was a ruler. All she had to do was repeat this procedure until she found a Medusan ruler.

However, there was a problem. Medusa's atmosphere was poisonous to people from the planet Earth, and Captain Temple therefore wore a closed helmet with an air supply attached to it. (Don't worry! The helmet did not interfere with her hearing.) She had been very eager to leave her ship and start looking for Medusans, so she had forgotten to check her air supply before she left the ship. Unfortunately, there was a slow leak in the air supply, so it was important for Captain Temple to find a Medusan ruler and get back to her ship as soon as possible.

Soon after she had discovered the leak in her air supply, Captain Temple saw two Medusans sitting under a tree. They looked exactly the same, as she

had expected. She ran over to them, and spoke to the one on her left. "Excuse me. Are you a ruler or a servant?" She asked.

The Medusan to whom she had spoken answered almost immediately. However, Captain Temple could not hear him (No! It had nothing to do with her helmet!) because a large bird flew overhead at that moment, making a loud noise. Therefore, she decided to speak to the Medusan on her right. She asked him, "Did that Medusan say he was a ruler or a servant?"

The second Medusan answered as quickly as the first had, and fortunately no bird flew overhead this time. He said, "He said that he is a ruler."

Captain Temple had been watching the gauge that measured her air supply for the past minute or so, and she realized that she had to act quickly. Her air supply was getting dangerously low. It was important for her to decide quickly whether either of these Medusans was a member of the ruling class. Did she have enough information to decide? Was she going to need to ask more questions before she knew whether she had found one of the rulers, or had she definitely found one already?

1. Suppose that the first Medusan was a servant. What must he have said? Why?

_____

_____

_____

2. Suppose that he was a ruler. What must he have said? Why?

_____

_____

_____

3. Whether he was a servant or a ruler, what must he have said? Why?

_____

_____

_____

4. Could either a servant or a ruler have said, "I am a ruler"? Why not?

_____

_____

_____

5. When the second Medusan said that the first had said, "I am a ruler," might he have been telling the truth or must he have been lying? How do you know?

_____

_____

_____

6. From the information she had, could Captain Temple have figured out what the first Medusan was? Why not?

_____

_____

_____

7. Could she have figured out what the second Medusan was? Why?

_____

_____

_____

8. Had Captain Temple found a member of the Medusan ruling class, or was she going to have to run back to her ship, get more air, and try again?

_____

_____

_____

Now, answer these questions.

1. Which modal perfect is used to show certainty about the past?

   would have _____

   might have _____

   must have _____

2. Which two modal perfects are used to show past possibility?

   would have _____

   should have _____

   might have _____

   could have _____

   must have _____

3. Which negative modal perfect is used to show past impossibility?

   should not have _____

   could not have _____

   might not have _____

D. *So . . . That*

> Sentences that contain *so . . . that* contain two clauses. The first clause contains *so* followed by an adjective or adverb. The second, the **result clause**, begins with *that*.

Clause Containing *So* Followed by an Adjective or Adverb	Result Clause Beginning with *That*
Jesse Owens was so nervous	that he thought he might foul again.

Sentences of this type can be thought of as coming from two sentences, one that contains an adjective or an adverb, and another that describes a result. This sentence can be thought of as coming from:

Jesse Owens was very nervous.
Therefore, he thought that he might foul again.

EXERCISE: Combine each pair of sentences to make one sentence that contains *so . . . that*. **The first one is done for you.**

1. Carmen wanted to please Richard very much.
   Therefore, she wore a miniskirt.
   Carmen wanted to please Richard so much that she wore a miniskirt.

2. Carmen's friends tried very hard to look young.
   Because of this, Carmen was uncomfortable with them.

   _____

   _____

3. Many people say that Carmen's face is very beautiful.
   Therefore, she has given other women the courage to stop dyeing their hair.

   _____

   _____

   _____

4. Lutz Long was very sportsmanlike.
   For this reason, he helped his opponent Jesse Owens.

   _____

   _____

5. Long was very eager to congratulate Owens.
   Therefore, he walked off the field arm-in-arm with his rival.

   _____

   _____

6. Owens was very grateful to Long.
   Consequently, he never forgot the German who had helped him.

   _____

   _____

7. Sarah was very relieved to see Tom.
   Therefore, she started waving and calling his name.

   _____

   _____

8. When Tom saw three people who needed his help, he was very confused.
   Consequently, he really didn't know what to do.

   _____

   _____

   _____

9. Captain Temple was very eager to look for Medusans.
   Therefore, she left her ship without checking her air supply.

   _____

   _____

   _____

10. She was very happy to see two Medusans.
    For that reason, she ran over to them.

    _____

    _____

From Chapter 4

A. Infinitives and Gerunds

■ 1. Perfect Infinitives and Gerunds

EXERCISE: With your partner, study the two groups of sentences and answer the questions that follow.

a. Mary started school about eighteen years ago. She graduated from college last June. At her college graduation, she cried when she remembered having gone to the school for the first time.

b. She is attending graduate school, and she is going to study for the next five years. When she finishes graduate school, she will get a doctorate and start teaching at a college or university. By the time she starts teaching, she expects to have been in school for about twenty-five years.

1. What verb form comes after the verb *remember* in the passage?

   an infinitive _____

   a gerund _____

2. What verb form comes after the verb *expect*?

   an infinitive _____

   a gerund _____

3. In the third sentence in group (a), what kind of gerund comes after *remembered*?

   a simple gerund _____

   a perfect gerund _____

4. In the third sentence in group (b), what kind of infinitive comes after *expects*?

   a simple infinitive _____

   a perfect infinitive _____

5. Underline the perfect gerund in the third sentence in group (a).

   How many words does it contain? _____

   Which one is a gerund? _____

   Which one is a past participle? _____

6. In the third sentence in group (a), which occurred first?

   the time described by the whole sentence _____

   the action described by the perfect gerund _____

7. Underline the perfect infinitive in the third sentence in group (b).

   How many words does it contain? _____

   Write the two words that make up the infinitive.

   _____   _____

   Write the past participle. _____

8. In the third sentence in group (b), which will occur first?

   the time described by the whole sentence _____

   the situation described by the perfect infinitive _____

9. Why are forms like *having gone* called *perfect* gerunds?

   _____

10. Why are forms like *to have been* called *perfect* infinitives?

    _____

11. What do the present perfect, the past perfect, modal perfects, perfect
    gerunds, and perfect infinitives have in common?

    _____

EXERCISE: Fill in the blank in each passage with either the perfect
gerund or the perfect infinitive form of the verb in parentheses. The first
two are done for you.

1. Mary is attending graduate school now, but she remembers (worry) <u>having</u>

   <u>worried</u> about getting enough money to go there. She decided to apply to

   graduate school anyhow, and she also applied for a fellowship. The

   professors who wrote her letters of recommendation knew her (be)

   _____ an excellent student in their classes.

   Moreover, they enjoyed (have) _____ her as a

   student. Therefore, they recommended her highly. Now, Mary is happy

   (get) _____ the opportunity to go to graduate

   school on a fellowship.

2. Most politicians make promises when they are running for election. However, some of them do not keep their promises. For example, the governor of Mary's state promised to build a new library for the state university. Many people who voted for her expected the library (be)

_____ completed by now, but the money hasn't even been allocated for its construction. Recently, a reporter asked the governor about the library, and the governor denied (promise)

_____ to build one. However, many people who voted for her clearly remember her (promise) _____.

3. When both husband and wife have full-time jobs outside the home, the division of household chores can sometimes cause problems. For example, if the husband gets home later, he may expect his wife (prepare)

_____ dinner and have it waiting for him. If the wife gets home later, she may expect her husband (finish)

_____ certain chores by the time she gets there.

■ 2. Gerunds as Nouns

EXERCISE: Write sentences that contain gerunds made from the verbs or verb phrases listed below. Two are done for you.

be employed	go to school
bear children	have
cook	sew
get married	suffer
give	trade

1. Being employed outside the home may cause a woman to have fewer children.

2. Some women want to devote their lives to working rather than to having children.

3. _____

_____

4. _____

_____

5. _____

_____

6. _____

_____

7. _____

_____

8. _____

_____

9. _____

_____

10. _____

_____

■ **3. Infinitives in Sentences with "Empty" *It* as Subject**

EXERCISE: Change each sentence to one that has *it* as a subject and contains an infinitive. The first two are done for you.

1. Supporting a family costs a lot. It costs a lot to support a family.

2. Doing the housework takes James Broadnax a long time. It takes James Broadnax a long time to do the housework.

3. Finding enough time to work and raise children often seems impossible.

_____

_____

4. Finishing everything you have to do must feel good.

_____

_____

5. Taking care of small children requires a great deal of patience.

_____

_____

6. In the past, getting a good education was harder for women.

_____

_____

7. Raising children may look easy, but it isn't.

_____

_____

8. Getting a good education costs a lot of time and money.

_____

_____

9. Managing a home well may require greater flexibility than a full-time job allows.

_____

_____

10. Providing for old people requires more careful planning than many people realize.

_____

_____

B. *Each* and *Every*

EXERCISE: With your partner, study the sentences and answer the questions that follow.

Standard Written English	Normal Spoken English
I think that all parents worry about their children's education.	I think that all parents worry about their children's education.
Each woman has her own ideas about how many children she should have.	Each woman has their own ideas about how many children they should have.
Every child should be loyal to his or her parents.	Every child should be loyal to their parents.

1. Which sentences are the same in standard written English and normal spoken English?

    those that contain *all* _____

    those that contain *each* _____

    those that contain *every* _____

2. Which sentences are different in standard written English and normal spoken English?

    those that contain *all* _____

    those that contain *each* _____

    those that contain *every* _____

3. Write a description of the differences.

    _____

    _____

    _____

EXERCISE: Read each of the spoken English sentences. If the spoken form is the same as the standard written form, write "the same" in the space provided. If it is different, write the standard English equivalent in the space provided.

1. Everyone is entitled to their own opinion about family size.

   _____

   _____

2. All people have to make up their own minds about how many children to have.

   _____

   _____

3. Each family has their own way of dividing chores among their members.

   _____

   _____

4. Should countries develop policies about family size, or should they allow each individual to make up their own mind?

   _____

   _____

5. Every parent has to decide whether earning extra money is more important than staying home with their children.

   _____

   _____

C. Real Conditionals

EXERCISE: With your partner, study the sentences in the chart and answer the questions that follow.

Real Conditionals

Time	Question and Answer	Presupposition	Real Conditional Sentence
present	Does that child's mother have a full-time job?	Suppose she has a full-time job.	If she has a full-time job, she is probably very busy.
	. I'm not sure. Maybe she has a full-time job, and maybe she doesn't.	Suppose she doesn't have a full-time job.	If she doesn't have a full-time job, she may work part-time.
future	Will the population of that country continue to decline?	Assume it continues to decline.	If it continues to decline, there will not be enough workers.
	No one knows for sure. It may continue to decline, or it may gradually start to increase.	Assume it gradually starts to increase.	If it gradually starts to increase, there may be a housing shortage.
past	Did you remember to give your daughter money to buy lunch at school?	Assume I gave her money for lunch.	If I gave her money, she bought lunch and ate with her friends.
	I'm not sure. I think that I gave her money for lunch, but maybe I didn't. I got up late, and I was in such a rush getting ready for work that I don't remember. (Note: the time is now 2:00 p.m. Lunchtime has passed.)	Assume I didn't give her money for lunch.	If I didn't give her money, she might have borrowed it from one of her friends, or one of her friends might have given her something to eat.

1. When are real conditionals used?

    When the presupposition is possible, or when the speaker or writer is

    not sure whether or not it is true _____

When the presupposition is not possible, or when the speaker or writer is sure that it is not true _____

2. Which clause contains the presupposition?

the *if*-clause _____

the result clause _____

3. What is the tense of the result clause?

the same tense that is used for factual statements about the time of the sentence (present for the present; future for the future; past for the past) _____

a tense that is "one step" further into the past than the tense that is used for factual statements about the time of the sentence (past for the present; past perfect for the past) _____

4. In which time is the tense of the *if*-clause different from the tense of the result clause?

the present _____

the future _____

the past _____

5. Which tense is used in the *if*-clause of a real conditional sentence about the future? _____

■ 1. Present Real Conditionals

EXERCISE: Read each statement. Then answer each question with a complete sentence using *if*. (There are no specific correct answers.) The first one is done for you.

1. Suppose a husband and wife both work outside the home. Should they share the household chores? <u>If a husband and wife both work outside the home, they should share the household chores. OR If a husband and wife both work outside the home, they should not share the household chores.</u>

2. Suppose a country has a decreasing population. Is it a good idea to encourage immigration?

_____

_____

3. What if a woman has small children? Should she work outside the home?

_____

_____

4. Suppose both a mother and father work outside the home. Can they provide a good family life for their children?

_____

_____

5. Is it possible for a father to go to school full-time? What if his children are under five years old?

_____

_____

6. Suppose a father and mother with small children both work outside the home. Do they have enough time for themselves?

_____

_____

■ 2. Future Real Conditionals

EXERCISE: Complete each sentence so that it contains a future real conditional statement. The first two are done for you.

1. If the population of a country declines, <u>it will have fewer workers.</u>

2. Feminists will continue to protest <u>if politicians do not pay attention to the needs of women.</u>

3. If the population of the world continues to increase at the present rate,

_____

_____

4. People will find a way to solve the problem if _____

_____

5. If a daughter of mine wants to get married before finishing her education,

_____

_____

6. If a son of mine wants to get married before finishing his education,

_____

_____

7. If I have several daughters and no sons (or: If a friend of mine has
several daughters and no sons), _____

_____

8. If _____

_____

9. _____ will _____ if

_____

10. _____

_____

■ 3. Past Real Conditionals

EXERCISE: In the passage on his research, Dr. Okpala does not tell us
how the questionnaire was administered to the subjects. Perhaps he asked
them to write answers to written questions. Perhaps he asked them the
questions and recorded their answers in writing, or perhaps he used a tape
recorder. Perhaps he was alone with each subject when he asked the
questions, or perhaps someone else, such as the woman's husband, was
present. Do you think that these conditions affected the types of subjects he
was able to use or the types of answers that they gave? Since we do not
know the exact conditions under which the questionnaire was
administered, we can use **past real conditional** sentences to speculate on
what happened and what the effects were, must have been, or might have
been.

Complete each sentence to make a past conditional sentence. The first one
is done for you.

1. If Okpala asked his subjects to write answers to written questions, <u>all of
the women he interviewed must have been able to read and write.</u>

2. If he was alone with each subject when he asked the questions, _____

_____

3. His subjects probably felt comfortable if _____

_____

4. If he interviewed his subjects when their husbands were present, _____

   _____

5. If he interviewed his subjects when some other people were present, _____

   _____

6. If he wrote down their answers, _____

   _____

7. If he used a tape recorder, _____

   _____

FROM CHAPTER 5

A. Distinguishing Between Contrast and Support

EXERCISE: Decide whether the second sentence in each pair supports or contrasts with the first. If it supports the first one, rewrite it to begin with "For instance" or "For example." If it contrasts, rewrite it to begin with "However." The first two are done for you.

1. The man and his wife seemed to be constantly working for the *encomendero*.
   They felt as if they were always spinning and weaving cloth for him.
   For instance, they felt as if they were always spinning and weaving cloth for him.

2. He wanted to leave the village.
   He had to wait until he had returned the work done by all who had helped him.
   However, he had to wait until he had returned the work done by all who had helped him.

3. You may not realize how many steps were involved in making cloth in colonial Latin America.
   Before it was dyed, firewood had to be collected to boil the dye.

   _____

   _____

4. The man and his wife could have finished making the cloth more quickly.
   They had other work to do in the village.

   _____

   _____

5. Actually plowing the fields took a day or two.
   Preparing to plow took several extra days.

   _____

   _____

6. The people in the village depended on each other.
   They could not have plowed their fields without each other's help.

   _____

   _____

7. Different percentages of women are in the work force in each European
   country.
   Almost 60 percent of Danish women work, while fewer than 30 percent
   of Spanish women do so.

   _____

   _____

8. Many European women do outwork or work at home.
   There are no official statistics on how many are involved in these alternative work arrangements.

   _____

   _____

9. European women tend to work in lower-paying, less prestigious jobs.
   In the Irish electronics industry, almost all of the worst-paid jobs are held
   by women.

   _____

   _____

10. Having people work at home may provide economic advantages for
    businesses.
    They may not have to spend money on new factories.

    _____

    _____

EXERCISE: Complete the following sentences about the topic that you are doing research on.

1. Before I started my research, I believed that _____

_____.

However, _____

_____.

2. My research has taught me a great deal about _____

_____. For instance, _____

_____.

3. _____

_____. However, _____

_____.

4. _____

_____. For example, _____

_____.

B. Different Ways of Showing Contrast

EXERCISE: Draw a circle around the word or expression that indicates contrast in each of the sentences. Then underline the part of the sentence that shows the contrast. The first one is done for you.

1. All people should be treated equally. (However,) their differences cannot be ignored.

2. All people should be treated equally. On the other hand, their differences cannot be ignored.

3. While all people should be treated equally, their differences cannot be ignored.

4. Although all people should be treated equally, their differences cannot be ignored.

5. Even though all people should be treated equally, their differences cannot be ignored.

6. Despite their needing to be treated equally, people's differences cannot be ignored.

7. In spite of their needing to be treated equally, people's differences cannot be ignored.

EXERCISE: With your partner, write rules to describe how to use of each pair or group of connectors. In your rules, describe punctuation and where to put the connector in relation to the contrast. Also tell which group of connectors to use before a noun or gerund phrase and which to use before a sentence or clause.

1. However; On the other hand

Punctuation: _____

Position in relation to contrast: _____

_____

Use before: _____

_____

2. While; Although; Even though

Punctuation: _____

Position in relation to contrast: _____

_____

Use before: _____

3. In spite of; Despite

Punctuation: _____

Position in relation to contrast: _____

_____

Use before: _____

EXERCISE: Complete the following sentences about the topic that you are doing research on.

1. While _____ say that _____

_____, I have

learned that _____.

2. _____ despite _____

_____.

3. _____

_____. On the other hand, _____

_____.

4. Although _____, _____

_____.

5. _____

_____. However, _____

_____.

6. _____

in spite of _____.

7. Even though _____, _____

_____.

C. The Passive Voice

EXERCISE: Work with your partner. Study the chart that follows. Complete the chart with examples of your own, and answer the questions that follow.

Active Sentence	Passive Equivalent
Present Continuous:	
Right now, farm workers all over the world *are producing* food.	Right now, food *is being produced* all over the world.
Simple Present:	
Many people in North and South America *speak* Native American languages.	Native American languages *are spoken* in North and South America.
Simple Past:	
The Spanish *invaded* Latin America in the sixteenth century.	Latin America *was invaded* in the sixteenth century.
Present Perfect:	
Many factors *have added* women to the labor force.	Women *have been added* to the labor force.
Simple Modal:	
We *must do* something about inequality.	Something *must be done* about inequality.
Past Progressive:	
_____ _____ _____	_____ _____ _____
Past Perfect:	
_____ _____ _____	_____ _____ _____
Modal Perfect:	
_____ _____ _____	_____ _____ _____

1. What word in the active sentence becomes the subject of the passive sentence?

   the subject _____   the object _____   the adjective _____

2. What form of the main verb is used in the passive sentence?

   the simple form _____   the past form _____

   the *-ing* form _____   the past participle _____

3. What verb comes before the past participle in the passive sentence?

   to be _____   *to have* _____   the main verb _____

4. Which verb in the passive sentence has the same tense as the main verb in the active sentence?

   to be _____

   the verb that comes from the main verb in the active sentence _____

EXERCISE: Change each active sentence into its passive equivalent. The first one is done for you.

1. The villagers spun raw cotton into yarn, dyed it, and wove it. <u>Raw cotton was spun into yarn, dyed, and woven.</u>

2. They collected firewood to boil the dye. _____

   _____

3. Some people prepared the food while others were plowing the fields.

   _____

   _____

4. European employers employ many women in the service sector. _____

   _____

5. Consumer demand is creating new jobs every day. _____

   _____

6. The schools have given European girls good educations, but the economy has not given women good jobs. _____

   _____

7. People used to perform more work at home. _____

   _____

8. People sell many crafts to tourists. _____

_____

9. Companies can build fewer factories because they recruit women to work
at home. _____

_____

10. Will employers continue to pay many women off the books? _____

_____

We use passive sentences when we want to focus on the object of an active sentence. For this reason, the subject of the active sentence is often not mentioned in the passive sentence. (This is the case with the passive sentences in the chart on page 314.)

Sometimes, however, we want to tell who or what performed the action. We can't use the subject of a passive sentence to do this, but we can use a *by*-phrase which contains the preposition *by* and the *agent*. The agent is the same noun or noun phrase that would be the subject of an active sentence. (*Agent* is a grammatical term for actor.)

EXERCISE: Study the chart. Then fill in the blanks in the box that follows.

Active Sentence	Passive Sentence with Agentive Phrase
Economic pressures are eroding the status of Chinese working women.	The status of Chinese working women is being eroded *by economic pressures*.
Spaniards invaded Latin America in the sixteenth century.	Latin America was invaded *by Spaniards* in the sixteenth century.
New consumer demands have created new jobs.	New jobs have been created *by new consumer demands*.

In a passive sentence that contains an agentive phrase, the subject of the corresponding active sentence is the _____ of the preposition _____ in the agentive phrase.

The _____ of the main verb in the active sentence becomes the subject of the passive sentence.

EXERCISE: Change each active sentence into a passive equivalent that contains a *by*-phrase. The first one is done for you.

1. Some European employers are encouraging alternative work arrangements. Alternative work arrangements are being encouraged by some European employers.

2. In China, new arrangements have eased the burden of maternity costs.

    _____

    _____

3. Formerly, only the woman's employer paid for maternity costs. _____

    _____

4. Some people claim that employers are dismissing women who take maternity leave. _____

    _____

5. An absence of seven years can make a worker uncompetitive. _____

    _____

6. By the time World War II was over, American women had taken over many of the men's jobs in the civilian work force. _____

    _____

7. Men reclaimed many, but not all, of these jobs. _____

    _____

D. Reduced Adjective Clauses That Contain Present and Past Participle Adjectives

EXERCISE: Rewrite each sentence by reducing the adjective clause. Your reduced clause should contain either a present participle or a past participle. The first two are done for you.

1. The people who lived in the village had to work for the encomendero.
   The people living in the village had to work for the encomendero.

2. A significant amount of the food that was grown in the village was given to the encomendero.
   A significant amount of the food grown in the village was given to the encomendero.

3. The language that was spoken in the village in colonial times was probably not Spanish.

   _____

   _____

4. The people who were working in the fields expected their labor to be returned.

   _____

   _____

5. The firewood that was collected by the man and his wife was used to boil the dye.

   _____

   _____

6. The schedule that was required by the encomendero did not allow the man to assign his own work.

   _____

   _____

7. In the Irish electronics industry, the people who do the best-paid jobs tend to be men.

   _____

   _____

8. Work that is performed outside company premises is called outwork.

_____

_____

With your partner compare the pairs of sentences on the left side of the chart with those on the right. Then complete the sentences in the box that follows to describe when present and past participles can come after the noun and when they must precede it as most adjectives do.

Participle Comes after the Noun in Reduced Clause	Participle Comes Before the Noun in Reduced Clause
Portuguese is a language *that is spoken in Europe and Latin America.*	Spanish is a language *that is spoken*, but Latin is not.
Portuguese is a language *spoken in Europe and Latin America.*	Spanish is a *spoken* language, but Latin is not.
The number of women *who have small children and work* has increased.	The number of women *having small children and working* has increased.
The number of women *who work* has increased.	The number of *working* women has increased.

When a present or past participle is part of a phrase that contains two or more words, it comes _____ the noun that it modifies.

When a present or past participle is not part of a phrase that contains two or more words, it comes _____ the noun that it modifies.

EXERCISE: Rewrite each sentence by reducing the adjective clause. Your reduced clause should contain either a present participle or a past participle. You will also have to decide whether the participle should come before or after the noun. The first two are done for you.

1. The pressures that are eroding women's status in the Chinese work force are economic.

   <u>The pressures eroding women's status in the Chinese workforce are economic.</u>

2. Profits that are maximized will put a company in a more competitive position.

   <u>Maximized profits will put a company in a more competitive position.</u>

3. The Chinese women who have been released in job rationalization drives may not find other jobs easily.

   _____

   _____

4. The numbers of service jobs, which are increasing, may be giving greater employment opportunities to women.

   _____

   _____

5. Female labor force participation rates that dipped during child-bearing years used to cause employers to feel justified in discriminating against women.

   _____

   _____

6. The gap that has narrowed between the percentages of males and females who are employed has changed the character of the work force of the United States.

   _____

   _____

FROM CHAPTER 6

<u>Unreal or Hypothetical Conditionals</u>

EXERCISE: Work with your partner. Study the sentences in the chart. Then answer the questions that follow.

Unreal or Hypothetical Conditionals

Time	Question and Answer	Presupposition	Unreal Conditional Sentence
present	Do men and women have the same roles in your culture? No, they don't.	Suppose they had the same roles.	If men and women had the same roles in my culture, they could share taking care of children.
	Are mothers in your culture usually responsible for taking care of babies? Yes, they are.	Suppose they weren't responsible for taking care of babies.	If mothers were not responsible for taking care of babies in my culture, I'm not sure what would happen.
future	Will people ever completely eliminate families? No, they will not.	Suppose they were to completely eliminate families. OR Suppose they completely eliminated families.	If people were to completely eliminate families, there wouldn't be anyone to raise the children. If people completely eliminated families, there wouldn't be anyone to raise the children.
past	Did Confucianism spread from China to Korea? Yes, it did.	Suppose it had not spread to Korea.	If Confucianism had not spread to Korea, the family might not have become so important there.
	Did Confucius teach that men and women should have the same roles? No, he did not.	Suppose he had taught that men and women should have the same roles.	If Confucius had taught that men and women should have the same roles, the structure of the family in many Asian countries might have developed very differently.

1. When are unreal conditionals used?

   When the presupposition is possible, or when the speaker or writer is not sure whether or not it is true _____

   When the presupposition is not possible, or when the speaker or writer is sure that it is not true _____

2. Which clause contains the presupposition?

   the *if*-clause _____

   the result clause _____

3. What is the tense of the result clause?

   the same tense that is used for factual statements about the time of the sentence (present for the present; future for the future; past for the past) _____

   a tense that is "one step" further into the past than the tense that is used for factual statements about the time of the sentence (past for the present; past or *were* plus infinitive for the future; past perfect for the past) _____

4. Are the tenses always different in unreal conditional sentences about the present and those about the future?

   yes _____   no _____

▪ 1. Present Unreal Conditionals

EXERCISE: Read each statement. Then answer each question with a complete sentence using *if*. (There are no specific correct answers.) There is a sample answer to the first question but there is also room for your answer.

1. Suppose that you could make only one change in the way your family does things. What one change would you make?
   If I could make only one change in the way my family does things, I would change the way that we make decisions.

   _____

   _____

2. Suppose you made this one change. What else would be different?

   _____

   _____

3. Suppose men and women had exactly the same roles in your culture? What would happen?

_____

_____

4. Suppose their roles were exactly the opposite. What might happen?

_____

_____

5. Suppose all countries had the same culture. Would the world be a better place or a worse place?

_____

_____

■ 2. Future Unreal Conditionals

EXERCISE: Complete each sentence so that it contains a future unreal conditional statement. The first two are done for you.

1. If we were all to try to help young people, there would be fewer problems in the world.

2. People's frustrations might decrease if they were given more choices about their roles in society.

3. If the number of extended families were to increase in the future, _____

_____

4. People might become much happier _____

_____

5. If the population of the world were to decrease, _____

_____

6. The world would become a better place to live in _____

_____

7. If I were to choose the kind of family structure I would prefer, _____

_____

8. If _____

_____

9. _____ would _____ if

_____

10. _____

_____

■ 3. Past Unreal Conditionals

EXERCISE: Complete each sentence to make a past conditional sentence. The first one is done for you.

1. If Confucius had not developed his philosophy, <u>the development of many Asian countries might have been very different.</u>

2. If Korea had not had close relations with China in the past, _____

_____

3. Would Confucius have developed a different philosophy if _____

_____

_____?

4. If the economic and social structure of Mexico had not changed, _____

_____

5. If Leopoldo Gomez had not been such a successful businessman, _____

_____

6. If _____

_____

7. _____ if _____

_____

Glossary

This section contains an alphabetical glossary of words that many students who use this text will not be familiar with. The number in parentheses after each entry indicates the chapter in which the word is first encountered.

This glossary does not contain every word that individual students will find difficult. I encourage students to use the personal glossary at the end of each chapter to keep a record of other words that they have needed help with understanding.

Abolition *Abolition* is the noun form of the verb *abolish*. To abolish a law or custom is to make it not exist any longer. (6)

Adopted *Adopted* children are not the biological children of a couple. They were born to different people but live in the family with all of the normal rights and responsibilities of biological children. (6)

Advent The *advent* of something means its coming or starting. (5)

Affiliation *Affiliation* is a connection with, or membership in, a group. (6)

Afforded In this context, *afforded* means made available. (6)

Allegedly If something is *alleged*, it is said to be true but it has not been proven. *Allegedly* is the adverb form. (4)

All the rage *All the rage* means extremely popular. (3)

Antithetical *Antithetical* means completely opposite. (6)

Arbitrary *Arbitrary* means determined by preference or convenience, rather than by necessity or nature. (6)

Armed forces The *armed forces* are the army, navy, marines, and other military groups. (5)

Ash *Ash* is all that is left after wood or other organic material has been burned. (3)

Astonish To *astonish* means to surprise greatly. The present participle is *astonishing*. (2)

Attachment In this context, *attachment* means connection. (5)

Backward *Backward* means not developed. (6)

Beforehand *Beforehand* means ahead of time. (1)

Bench A *bench* is a shaped like a long, low table. Some *benches* are to sit on, but a *work bench* is to do work on. (2)

Benefits When workers receive health insurance and other kinds of payment in addition to money, these other kinds of payment are called *(fringe)* *benefits. Benefits* include health insurance, being paid when one does not work on holidays, and being paid when one is sick. (4)

Bias   *Bias* in this context means prejudice. (6)

Boston Magazine   *Boston Magazine* is a monthly magazine about Boston and places near Boston. Once a year, the magazine publishes an article on the best places for different things. (2)

Bound   In this context, *bound* means limited. (4)

Buick   A *Buick* is a kind of American car. (4)

Bracket   In this context, a *bracket* is a group defined by being between two numbers in a series. (5)

Branches   *Branches* are parts of a large family. They are usually begun by brothers or sisters. The idea of a branch comes from thinking of the family as a tree. (6)

Break   In this context, a *break* is a change which makes things easier. A *tax break* is a reduction in taxes. (4)

Burden   A *burden* is something that one carries. It is also a duty or responsibility. (5)

Cast iron   *Cast iron* is iron that has been poured as a hot liquid into a container that has a certain shape. When the iron cools and becomes hard, it is taken out. Many old wood stoves were made of cast iron. (2)

Casual   A *casual* employee is someone whose job is occasional or temporary. Such an employee can usually be fired at any time. (5)

Cease   To *cease* means to stop. (6)

Chaos   *Chaos* is complete confusion and disorganization. (4)

Channel   To *channel* information is to send it on the correct path to reach the place where it should go. (6)

Charm   Something that is attractive has *charm*. (2)

Chores   *Chores* are regular jobs that must be done at home. (4)

Christening   A *christening* is a ritual in Christian religions during which a baby is given his or her name. (6)

Cite   In this context, to *cite* means to blame. (4)

Civilian   *Civilian* is the opposite of military. Someone who is a *civilian* is not in the armed forces. (5)

Clerk   A *clerk* is usually someone who works in an office. The adjective form of this noun is *clerical*. (4)

Cohabiting   *Cohabiting* means living together. (6)

Coincide   If two events occur at the same time, they *coincide* with each other. (5)

Common   In this context, *common* means shared. (4)

Compatible   *Compatible* means able to exist together. *Incompatible* is the negative form of this adjective.

Comply   To *comply* means to obey. (5)

Compound   In this context, a *compound* is a group of houses that is separated from other houses, often by a fence or a wall. (6)

Compulsory   *Compulsory* means required. (6)

Concentrate on   To *concentrate on* something is to pay full attention to it. (2)

Concerning   In this context, *concerning* means about. (4)

Confucius   *Confucius* was a respected philosopher who lived and taught in China. Scholars believe that he was born in 551 B.C. and died in 479 B.C. His teaching emphasized the importance of relationships within the family and society. *Confucian* philosophy has been very important in Korea and other east Asian countries. (6)

Conserved   *Conserved* means saved without any loss. (1)

Considerable   *Considerable* means significant. (6)

Consistent   To be *consistent* means to be regular, without variation. The adverb form of this adjective is *consistently*. (4)

Constitute   To *constitute* means to form or make up. (6)

Constrained   In this context, *constrained* means prevented or stopped. (4)

Construed   To be *construed* as something means to be believed to be that thing. (6)

Contend   To *contend* is to make a strong statement. (4)

Contretemps   A *contretemps* is an argument. (3)

Convergence   To *converge* means to come together. *Convergence* is the noun form of this verb. (5)

Council   A *council* is a group that meets regularly for a specific purpose. (4)

Craft   A *craft* is the activity of making something by hand. (5)

Cues   *Cues* in this context are signals to act in a certain way. (6)

Culinary   The adjective *culinary* refers to things that are cooked or otherwise prepared in a kitchen to be eaten. (2)

Cultivated   *Cultivated* means given nourishment and otherwise taken care of. (6)

Day-care   *Day-care* is caring for children while their parents are working. (4)

Delta   *Delta* is the fourth letter of the Greek alphabet. It is shaped like a triangle. A *delta* is the area where a river divides into several streams as it flows into a lake or sea. (2)

Determinant   A *determinant* is something that influences a result. (6)

Dinosaurs   *Dinosaurs* were large animals that lived on the earth millions of years ago. (1)

Dip   To *dip* means to go down or to decrease. (5)

Disaster   A *disaster* is something that causes great damage or loss. (5)

Discordant   The adjective *discordant* is a word that originally applies to music. It means not in harmony, not pleasant sounding. It can also be applied to sights and ideas. (2)

Disgrace   *Disgrace* is a strong form of shame. (6)

Dismiss   To *dismiss* a worker is to take away his or her job. (5)

Display case   A *case* is a box for holding something. A *display case* is made out of glass so that it can *display*, or show, what it contains. *Display cases* are common in stores. (2)

Disturb   To *disturb* is to cause not to feel peaceful. (2)

Divergent   *Divergent* means differing. (6)

Diverse   *Diverse* means different from one another. (6)

Drive   A *drive* is an organized effort. Thus, a *rationalization drive* is an organized effort to make things more reasonable. (5)

Edge further down   To *edge further down* means to CONTINUE decreasing slowly. (5)

Elapses   Time *elapses* means times passes. (5)

Embrace   In this context, to *embrace* means to include. (4)

Encomendero   In colonial Latin America, an *encomendero* was a Spaniard who was entitled to receive labor and goods from a group of Indians he had been "given" by the king or queen. (5)

Encompass   To *encompass* means to include. (5)

Encyclopedia   An *encyclopedia* is a set of books containing general information. (1)

Endowments   *Endowments* are natural abilities. (6)

Enlarge   To *enlarge* something is to make it bigger. (2)

Ensuing   *Ensuing* means following, coming after. (5)

Enterprise   An *enterprise* is a business. (5)

Entrepreneur   An *entrepreneur* is a businessperson, usually someone who owns his or her own business. The word has been borrowed from French. (6)

Erode   To *erode* is to slowly destroy or make smaller. The basic meaning of *erode* is physical. It refers to the action of wind, water, and other natural forces in changing the shape of beaches, mountains, and other natural features. (5)

Ethic   An *ethic* is a moral value. (6)

Evident   *Evident* means noticeable, obvious, easy to see. (5)

Excess   *Excess* means extra, not needed. (5)

Extinct   When a group of animals or people becomes *extinct*, there are no more members of that group alive. (4)

Extirpate   To *extirpate* is to destroy completely. (6)

Exuberant   *Exuberant* means happy, full of life, enthusiastic. (2)

Facilitate   To *facilitate* means to make easier or possible. (6)

Factor   In this context, a *factor* is a characteristic. (4)

Feminists   *Feminists* are people who believe that the sexes should have equal rights and be treated equally. They often organize in order to work for women's rights. (4)

Fertile   Land that is *fertile* produces crops easily. (2)

Flexibility   *Flexibility* means the ability to change according to new or different requirements. (5)

Follow in someone's footsteps   To *follow in someone's (usually a parent's) footsteps* is an idiomatic expression. It means to follow the same profession or do the same things that that person did. (6)

Foregone conclusion   A *foregone conclusion* is something that everyone expects to happen. (3)

Foul   To *foul* is to violate a rule of correct movement in a sport. In this case, Jesse Owens did not start his jump from the correct area. (3)

Fulfillments   *Fulfillments* are satisfactions. (4)

Gamut   *Gamut* means range. It includes all members of a set. (6)

Gap   A *gap* is a space that separates two groups or things. (5)

Get-together   A *get-together* is an informal party. (6)

Gradual   *Gradual* means happening slowly. (5)

Greengrocer   A *greengrocer* is someone who sells fresh fruits and vegetables. (6)

Gustave Flaubert   *Gustave Flaubert* was a famous French writer. (2)

Hairdressing   *Hairdressing* means cutting, washing, curling, or otherwise fixing a person's hair. (4)

Hard-headed   To be *hard-headed* means to be stubborn. (6)

Householder   *Householder* is a term for the person who is the head of a family or household. (6)

Housework   *Housework* consists of chores that are done at home. It is not the same as homework. (4)

Hydroplane   A *hydroplane* is an airplane that can land on water. (2)

Ideology   An *ideology* is a way of thinking that is common to a group or culture. It often applies to political beliefs. (6)

Ill-fitting   Something that fits is the right size and shape. Something that is *ill-fitting* does not fit well. (6)

Imposed   People are forced to follow rules that are *imposed*. (6)

Incentive   An *incentive* is something that makes people want to act in a certain way. It is a kind of reward. (4)

Indelible   Something that is *indelible* cannot be erased. (6)

Inferior   *Inferior* means less important or powerful. (6)

Infernally   In this context, *infernally* means annoyingly. (2)

Inner city   The *inner city* is the older center of a city. It usually has many people living in it in comparison with its size, and the majority of these people are usually poor. (6)

Institution   An *institution* is an important tradition, practice, or organization in a society. (6)

Integrated   In this context, to be *integrated* means to participate equally in a group or society. (5)

Intrafamily/Interfamily   *Intra-* means within. *Inter-* means between or among. *Intrafamily* means within the same family. *Interfamily* means between or among two or more families. In the passage, a hyphen is used after *intra* to show that it also modifies *family*. (6)

Inverted   To *invert* something is to turn it upside down. The past participle of this verb is *inverted*. (5)

Ivy League   The *Ivy League* schools are a group of fairly old colleges in the eastern United States that are respected both academically and socially. (6)

Jostle   To *jostle* is to push other people (or animals) in order to get where you want to go. (2)

Jump   In this context, to *jump* means to increase quickly. (5)

Kinship   *Kinship* means family relationship. (6)

Labor-intensive   A *labor-intensive* business is one that requires many hours of work. (6)

Lament   A *lament* is an expression of sorrow. (4)

Large-scale   *Large-scale* means very big. (6)

Leave   If a worker is permitted to leave his or her job for a period of time and then to return to it, that worker has been given a *leave*. A *leave* is a fringe benefit. (5)

Life cycle   The *life cycle* refers to the different stages that a person goes through in his or her life. For example, the teenage years are part of the life cycle. (5)

Load   A *load* is something that is carried, either physically or mentally. (4)

Long-standing   Something that has existed for a long time can be called *long-standing*. (5)

Lore   *Lore* means traditional knowledge or belief that is passed down from parent to child. (2)

Magnitude   *Magnitude* means size. (1)

Medieval   The Middle Ages, or *medieval* times, were the period from the fall of Rome (approximately 500 A.D.) to the (re-)discovery of North and South Americas by Europeans (approximately 1500 A.D.). (2)

Memorabilia   *Memorabilia* are things that are important to remember. (6)

Memorial tablets   A *Memorial tablet* is a flat piece of stone on which the name and other information about someone (usually someone who has died) are written. (6)

Metropolis   A *metropolis* is a the most important city in a region, usually the capital city of a state or country. (2)

Millenium   A *millenium* is a period of 1000 years. (4)

Minor   Something that is *minor* is not very important. (4)

Miniskirt   A *miniskirt* is a very short skirt. This style was popular for women in many western countries during the 1960s. (3)

MIT   The initials *MIT* stand for the Massachusetts Institute of Technology, a famous university in Cambridge, Massachusetts. (1)

Mixer   A *mixer* is a machine that combines (mixes) things together. Electric *mixers* are kitchen appliances. (2)

Mortgage   A *mortgage* is a loan that is taken to buy a house. (4)

Moulded   *Moulded* means shaped. The spelling is British. The American English spelling is *molded*. (6)

Mutual   *Mutual* means exchanging advice, help, or other things. It is similar in meaning to *reciprocal*. If there is *mutual* assistance, people help each other. (6)

Network   A *network* is a system of relationships. (6)

Noble   A *noble* has inherited importance or power. In this context, *common* is the opposite of *noble*. (6)

Noblesse oblige   *Noblesse oblige* is an expression borrowed from French. It means "nobility obliges." This means that a person's high position requires him or her to behave generously towards those who are poorer or weaker. (6)

Normative   *Normative* is a term used by sociologists and psychologists. It refers to behavior that is accepted and required by a society. (6)

Norm   A *norm* is an average, an accepted way of being in a particular society or group. (5)

Nursing homes   In some cultures, sick or old people are sent to *nursing homes* where they are taken care of (or nursed) by people who are not members of their families. (6)

Obsolete   Something (or someone) that has been made useless by modern technology or changes is *obsolete*. (5)

Off the books   When people are paid *off the books*, the government and other agencies are not informed about their working. Therefore, the employee may not have to pay taxes, but he or she does not receive official protection. (5)

Offspring   *Offspring* means child or children. (6)

On hold   *On hold* means waiting to be put into action. (4)

Operation   In this context, an *operation* means a business. (2)

Outlook   An *outlook* is a point of view, a perspective. (5)

Outright   *Outright* means completely. (5)

Outsider   An *outsider* is a stranger, someone who does not belong to a particular group. (6)

Paramount   *Paramount* means more important than anything else. (6)

Participation   To *participate* in something means to be active in it. *Participation* is the noun form of this verb. *Participation* in the labor force means working. (5)

Particle   A *particle* is a very small piece of something. (1)

Patrons   In this context, *patrons* are customers. (2)

Peasants   *Peasants* are common people who work on the land. (6)

Penalize   To *penalize* means to punish. (6)

Perpetuate   To *perpetuate* means to cause to continue. (5)

Persist   To *persist* means to continue. (4)

Pertain   To *pertain* to something means to be appropriate to something. (6)

Pigeons   *Pigeons* are birds that often live in cities. (2)

Plow   To *plow* means to prepare the ground for planting by breaking up the soil. (5)

Plummet   In this context, to *plummet* means to decrease quickly. (5)

Policy   A *policy* is a specific method of action that has been selected. (4)

Potentiality   A *potentiality* is an ability to develop or exist. (6)

Pottery   *Pottery* is dishes or other containers that are made out of clay that has been dried or baked. (2)

Preassigned   *Preassigned* means assigned or decided upon earlier. (6)

Predict   To *predict* is to say what will happen in the future. (4)

Premises   Company *premises* include both the company's land and the buildings that are on it. (5)

Prestigious   *Prestigious* means valued highly by other people. (5)

Presuppose   To *presuppose* something means to assume that it exists. (6)

Preservation   *Preservation* is the noun form of the verb *to preserve*. To *preserve* means to save or protect. (6)

Prevalence   *Prevalence* is the noun form of the adjective *prevalent*. Something that is *prevalent* is very common. (6)

Prevalent   *Prevalent* means very common or accepted. (5)

Prewar   The prefix *pre-* means before. In this context, *prewar* means before World War II. (4)

Prime   *Prime* means first, most important. (5)

Primordial   *Primordial* means basic. (6)

Princeton   *Princeton* University is one of the Ivy League schools. It is located in New Jersey, the state southeast of New York. (6)

Product   A *product* is a result, something that is produced. (5)

Profound   *Profound* means deep, important. (5)

Prominent   *Prominent* means obvious, noticeable. (5)

Propaganda   *Propaganda* is a kind of advertising designed to change people's beliefs. (4)

Propagation   *Propagation* is the noun form of the verb to *propagate*. To propagate means to make grow. (6)

Proportions   In this context, *proportion* means size as compared with other sizes. The phrase *unmanageable proportions*, which means that something is too big to manage, is used quite often. (6)

Prosper   To *prosper* is to succeed economically. (5)

Pulsate   To *pulsate* is to move in rhythm, like the heart. (2)

Quaintness   When something is *quaint*, it is unusual or different. *Quaintness* is the noun formed from this adjective. (2)

Radical   *Radical* groups are groups that want to make great changes in the society in which they live. (6)

Rate   In this context, a *rate* is a proportion or percentage. (5)

Rationalization   To *rationalize* means to make more reasonable. *Rationalization* is the noun form of this verb. (5)

Raw   *Raw* means in a natural state, and not processed. (5)

Rebound   To *rebound* means to come back to the original position. (5)

Reciprocal   *Reciprocal* means alternating. It is similar in meaning to *mutual*. In a *reciprocal* relationship, each person has obligations to the other, but the obligations may be different. (6)

Redundant   In this context, *redundant* means more than necessary. (5)

Reef   A *reef* consists of a chain of rocks that is near or on the surface of a body of water. Divers like to dive near *reefs* because there are often interesting fish there. (2)

Regime   In this context, a *regime* is a kind of schedule.

Relative to   In this context, *relative to* means compared with. (4)

Relevant   *Relevant* means important to what is being discussed. (6)

Remarkable   *Remarkable* means very noticeable. (4)

Render   In this context, to *render* means to cause to be a certain way. (5)

Renew   To *renew* is to make like new again. (6)

Residual   *Residual* means remaining from the past. (4)

Respondent   Someone who answers (or *responds* to) a questionnaire can be called a *respondent*. (4)

Reverse   To *reverse* is to turn in the opposite direction. (5)

Rid of   To *rid* A *of* B is to remove B from A. Chinese businesses have been removing excess labor. (5)

Rigors   *Rigors* are difficult aspects of life. (4)

Ritual   A *ritual* is a special ceremony, such as a wedding or a funeral. (6)

Rugged   *Rugged* means strongly built, or made up of strong parts. The phrase *rugged individualism* is a fairly common one. It refers to the belief that individuals must stand up for what they believe in even if others do not agree. (6)

Ruins   *Ruins* are what remains of old cities and buildings. (2)

Saint's day   A *saint's day* is the day on which a particular saint (holy person) is remembered. In the Roman Catholic religion, each person has a saint who is important to him or her, and the celebration of this saint's day is also important to him or her. (6)

Scenario   In this context, a *scenario* is a short summary of what may happen. (5)

Scold   To *scold* means to tell someone, often in a loud voice, that he or she has not behaved well. (6)

Scuba divers   To *dive* is to jump into water head first, and often to swim under it. People who *dive* are called *divers*. *Scuba divers* are divers who wear *scuba* equipment, which allows them to stay under water for long periods. (2)

Second-hand   *Second-hand* means owned by someone else before. (4)

Sector   A *sector* is a part of a circle, shaped like a piece of pie. Economists divide the economy into different *sectors* according to the kinds of jobs that people perform. This usage comes from thinking of the whole economy, for example, as a circle. (5)

Self-appointed   People who are *self-appointed* to a particular role have chosen it for themselves without anyone else suggesting that they do so. (6)

Service   When person A works for person B without producing anything, person A performs a *service*. For example, cooking, cleaning, and serving food are services. (5)

Sexist   People who are *sexist* believe that all roles must be based on a person's sex. (4)

Shame   When people are ashamed, they feel *shame*. (6)

Sharply   In this context, *sharply* means suddenly. (5)

Shift   A *shift* is a change, a movement. (5)

Six-to-three work schedule   Someone who has a *six-to-three work schedule* starts working at six in the morning and finishes at three in the afternoon. In the United States, a nine-to-five work schedule is considered the most common. (4)

Solidarity   *Solidarity* means unity. (6)

Solicited   If something is *solicited*, it is asked for. If it is *unsolicited*, it is not asked for.

Spin   To *spin* is to make fibers such as cotton into thread. (5)

Spinster   A *spinster* is a woman who has never gotten married. This word is more likely to be used in cultures in which everyone is expected to get married. (6)

Stamp   A *stamp* in this context means a special character that lasts for a long time. (6)

Stand on one's own feet   To *stand on one's own feet* is an idiomatic expression. It means to be independent. (6)

State   A *state* is a condition. Traditional physics describes three *states* of matter: solid, liquid, and gas. (1)

Status   Position in relation to others is called *status*. (5)

Steady   Something that is *steady* continues without stopping. (4)

Step up   To *step up* means to increase. (4)

Striking   *Striking* means obvious or very noticeable. (6)

Strive   To *strive* is to try very hard. (5)

Subcontract   Suppose that business A agrees to do some work for business B. If business A hires another person or business to do part of this work, business A is said to *subcontract* that part of the work. (5)

Subsist   To *subsist* is to continue to exist. (6)

Supersede   To *supersede* means to be more important. (6)

Surge   A *surge* is a sudden increase. (5)

Survival   To *survive* means to continue living. *Survival* is the noun form of this verb. (4)

Sweatshop   A *sweatshop* is a factory in which people work in unhealthy conditions for long hours and low pay. (5)

Switch   To *switch* means to move from one place to another, or to exchange. It is also a term used in speaking of electricity or the flow of information. The way the centralizing women are talked about in this passage uses the image of a computer network as a metaphor. (6)

Tabulation   In this context, a *tabulation* is another word for a table. (5)

Take-home pay   *Take-home pay* is what a worker earns after taxes. (4)

Temperamental   *Temperamental* means having moods or emotions which change quickly and unexpectedly. (6)

Tempered   *Tempered* means adjusted or made calmer. (6)

Tenet   A *tenet* is a basic belief or principle of a group or organization. (5)

Terminating   *Terminating* means causing to end. (6)

Textile   *Textile* means cloth. (5)

Thrill   To *thrill* is to excite. (2)

Toddlers   *Toddlers* are young children who are just beginning to walk. (5)

Townhouse   A *townhouse* is usually a two- or three-story house in which one family lives. It shares a wall with one or two other houses. (4)

Trace   In this context, to *trace* is to copy the outside shape of something with a line. (5)

Trading   In this context, *trading* refers to selling and other business activities. *Petty trading* means selling small goods and services. (4)

Transition   A *transition* is a change. (1)

Tribe   A *tribe* is a group of many related families. Mr. Aizawa is talking about the entire nation of Japan. (4)

Undergo   To *undergo* means to experience (usually something unpleasant). (6)

Unfounded   If there is not much evidence to support a belief, it is *unfounded*. (5)

Unisex   *Unisex* means being the same for males and females. (5)

Unmanageable   Something that is *manageable* can be controlled. Something that is *unmanageable* cannot be controlled. (6)

Unseemly   *Unseemly* means not suitable. It can apply to something that doesn't look right. (6)

Upkeep   *Upkeep* is the act or cost of keeping something in good condition. (4)

Upward mobility   *Upward mobility* refers to the ability of a person or group to raise his, her, or its position in society. (6)

Variety   In this context, *variety* means a kind or type. (5)

Virtually   *Virtually* means almost completely. (5)

Vitality   In this context, *vitality* means liveliness. (2)

Warp   The warp refers to a group of threads on a loom. (5)

Wayward   People who are *wayward* do not do what is expected of them. (6)

Wedding reception   A *wedding reception* is a party that is held after a wedding. (4)

Withdraw   To *withdraw* means to leave. (5)

Yarn   *Yarn* is thread that can be used to weave cloth. (5)